D1525755

WHY WAIT?
BE HAPPY NOW!

*Finding Your Path
to Unconditional Happiness*

DONNA DAISY PH.D.

No part of this publication may be reproduced
in whole or in part, or stored in a retrieval system,
or transmitted in any form or by any means,
electronic, mechanical, photocopying, recording,
or otherwise, without written permission of the author,
except for the inclusion of brief quotations in a review.
For information regarding permission, please write to:
info@barringerpublishing.com

Text and Illustrations copyright ©2010 by Donna Daisy
All rights reserved.

Barringer Publishing April 2010
Naples, Florida
www.barringerpublishing.com
Cover, graphics, layout design by Lisa Camp
Editing by Elizabeth Heath
Cover Photography by Kekoa Schlesinger

ISBN: 978-0-9825109-3-3

Library of Congress Cataloging-in-Publication Data
Why Wait? Be Happy Now! by Donna Daisy

Printed in U.S.A.

Dedication

This book is dedicated with love to my amazing children,
David, Kathy and Kim for their unfailing support and belief in me,
to the many friends who walked the walk with me,
and uplifted me daily through the four years of Charles' illness,
and to my dog, Abby, the true master of
unconditional happiness and love.

Acknowledgments

I would like to extend my deepest thanks to the following
people for assisting me in the creation of this book:
Jeff Schlesinger of Barringer Publishing for his
dedication and encouragement as we proceeded from a simple idea,
to a vision, to the actual manifestation of our dream—this book.
Elizabeth Heath for her patience, perseverance and excellent editorial skills.
Lisa Camp for the cover, graphics and layout design.

About the Author

As a psychologist, life coach, author, and professional speaker, Donna believes that the best way to predict the future is to create it. Donna's doctoral studies on resilience, clinical training in stress management at the Harvard Medical School Institute of Mind/Body Medicine, and studies in the field of Positive Psychology provide the background for her lecture's and her book, *Why Wait? Be Happy Now!*

Donna is also the author of *Rise Above It: Five Powerful Strategies for Overcoming Adversity and Achieving Success* as well as a regular contributor to articles appearing in many magazines and newspapers. In her coaching practice, books, lectures and workshops, Donna encourages others to embrace their personal power, make life changing choices, and take the necessary action to create the results they want in their lives.

For more information visit **www.donnadaisy.com**

Foreward

During my husband's illness, I happened to read a quote by Mahatma Gandhi which said, "Be the change you want to see in the world." I had heard that quote several times in the past, but it never touched me as deeply as it did at this time.

I realized that if I wanted happiness in my life, and if I wanted love in my life during these difficult times, I was going to have to be that happiness and I was going to have to be that love. So I undertook the task of training my mind for happiness and tuning my heart to love. I learned everything I could about how to think like happy people think, do what happy people do, and love like happy people love.

My background as a psychologist and life coach had prepared me well in the areas of attitude, knowledge and skills. What I had to do now, however, was consciously start living from my heart what I knew to be true in my head. My husband, Charles, had not been formally trained in happiness and resilience skills, yet he seemed to have mastered these things on his own. Together, we learned to live and love from a higher place during the four years he was ill. Day in and day out we learned more and more about the art of sustainable happiness.

In this book, I share with you the very personal and profound insights and strategies that lifted our spirits and our happiness level well above what we could have ever expected given the huge challenges we faced on a daily basis. Writing this book has been a therapeutic blessing in my life. May the information you find here and the feelings you experience be a blessing in your life as well.

With greatest love and respect for you,
Donna Daisy

THIS BOOK IS FOR INFORMATIONAL AND EDUCATIONAL PURPOSES ONLY AND DOES NOT CONSTITUTE ANY SERVICES OF A PROFESSIONAL MENTAL HEALTH PROVIDER OR ANY FORM OF THERAPY. READERS ARE ENCOURAGED TO SEEK OUT THE SERVICES OF A LICENSED PROFESSIONAL MENTAL HEALTH PROVIDER FOR AREAS OF THEIR LIVES WHERE THEY NEED PROFESSIONAL CARE. THE AUTHOR DOES NOT PROMISE OR GUARANTEE ANY LEVEL OF SUCCESS FROM THE IDEAS OR SUGGESTIONS PRESENTED. IN NO EVENT SHALL THE AUTHOR, PUBLISHER OR DISTRIBUTOR BE HELD LIABLE FOR ANY LOSS, RISK, DAMAGE, USE OR MISUSE OF ANY OF THE INFORMATION EITHER DIRECTLY OR INDIRECTLY PRESENTED HEREIN. THE OPINIONS CONTAINED IN THIS BOOK ARE BASED ON CLINICAL EXPERIENCE AND ARE THAT OF THE AUTHOR. ALL IDENTIFIABLE FACTS AND STORIES HAVE BEEN CHANGED TO PROTECT PATIENT CONFIDENTIALITY.

Table of Contents

PART 1

Training Your Mind for Happiness

INTRODUCTION

Think about how many times you have said to yourself, "I will be so happy when I retire in ten years. That is when life will really be good," or "I will be happy when I get a different job." Or when my husband gets his act together. Or when the kids grow up. Or when I get that promotion at work.

It is so easy to postpone today's happiness on the belief that when your situation changes, your level of happiness will also change. So often we believe that our circumstances—not us—are in control of how happy we are. In reality, our circumstances do not define our happiness. In the words of author and lecturer Dr. Wayne Dyer, "they just represent our unique curriculum—our tests, challenges and opportunities for personal growth." What does define our happiness is what we tell ourselves about our circumstances and the choices we make as a result.

I would like to share a personal story with you—the story of the four years of my life that led me to write this book. My husband, Charles, developed an infection in both of his legs, resulting in his confinement to a wheelchair and eventually, the amputation of his right leg. I became a full time caregiver as we worked together to manage his health issues. We both recognized that if we adopted the mindset that, "We will be happy when Charles gets better," or "We will be happy when Charles can walk again," we would miss the opportunity for many delightful moments and the closeness we often shared as we worked together to get through those challenging times. So rather than saying, "we'll be happy when," we chose a new motto: "Why wait? Be happy now!" We weren't going to allow our happiness to depend on conditions that were outside of our control. I lost my husband in September of 2009, but I will always cherish the choice we made to be happy together, right then, in the present moment. I believe that all of us are capable of long, rich, and satisfying life experiences. But the ability to remain happy, especially in times of adversity, requires the conscious use of some very specific skills, including choosing the perspective with which we view the things that happen to us. Each day, we all have a choice to be happy when, or to be happy now. This book is not a book of theories about how to be happy. It is about training your mind to think in a way that generates good feelings (Part I) and training your heart to function from a place of love (Part II). You will learn how to achieve and maintain happiness using very specific, well-researched strategies that worked for me even in my darkest moments and have proven successful for clients and readers of mine as well. It is about being happy now— unconditionally. It is about a sustainable happiness that can never be taken away because of a change in your circumstances. My desire—my goal—in writing this book, is to share with you the mindset, the heartset and the strategies that helped make each and every day of those four years of Charles' illness some of the best days of our life together. I am confident that as you read this book and come to better understand the incredible power you have to consistently live above the line that separates happiness from unhappiness, you will easily create the joyous, abundant and loving life you desire and deserve.

Admittedly, the idea that happiness is a choice,

rather than contingent on what is going on in your life

is a little daunting and takes some getting used to.

The payoff for accepting this belief, however, is huge.

CHAPTER 1

Out of My Mind

Most of the time, when I suggest to someone that it is possible to be happy all of the time, the response I get is, "Are you out of your mind?" People cite reasons like fear of job loss, the poor economy, money woes, a list of other worries as reasons they can't possibly maintain a happy state. Philosopher Peter Russell once said, "The sad joke about all human beings is that we spend so much time worrying about whether we are going to be happy in the future, we are never at peace in the present." In other words, we miss the opportunity to be happy now because we are afraid we won't be happy tomorrow.

THE CHOICE IS MADE BY YOU

As a life coach, I talk with a lot of people who are experiencing very little happiness or joy in their lives. I used to find myself wondering, "Are there basic differences between the people who are happy most of the time and those who are unhappy most of the time? And if so, what are those differences, and how do you overcome them if you are one of the unhappy ones?"

Over the last few years, I have come to realize that happiness (or unhappiness) isn't caused by other people in our lives. Nor is it caused by a particular set of circumstances. The choice to be happy or not is made by you, even though you may not always realize it.

UNCONDITIONAL HAPPINESS

Most of us are pretty well-entrenched in beliefs that tell us "happiness isn't possible until I get my health back" or "happiness isn't possible as long as I have to live in this crowded little apartment," or "happiness isn't possible until I find my soul-mate." The reality is that while each of those conditions that you place upon your happiness may represent a strong personal desire, none of them have the power to make you unhappy—unless you give them permission to do so.

Ask yourself this question: "Do I want to be happy?" When you can answer that question "yes" without any qualifiers (such as, "I will be happy just as soon as I lose thirty pounds"), then you are ready to experience unconditional happiness every minute of the day. You are ready to be happy, regardless of your circumstances.

Admittedly, the idea that happiness is a choice, rather than contingent on what is going on in your life is a little daunting and takes some getting used to. The payoff for accepting this belief, however, is huge. I recently met with a young woman—let's call her Sally—and listened to her story about all the things in her life that were preventing her from being happy. Her brothers verbally abused her since childhood, and even as adults, they are cruel, unkind, and emotionally distant when they communicate. Of her three adult children, only one maintains a warm and loving relationship with her. The others she rarely hears from. Both her mother and father, who adored her as a child, have passed away. Sally not only felt alienated from her family, she had extremely negative self-talk. She told herself, "I am worthless. It's all my fault that my brothers treat me the way they do." At times, Sally was so distraught that she believed the world would be better off without her. She was allowing her happiness to be robbed by her own negative thoughts and by the actions and opinions of others.

WHAT MATTERS IS YOUR PERSPECTIVE

What Sally had not yet realized was this: It's not what happens to you in life that matters. What matters is your perspective—what you tell yourself about what happens.

The perspective you choose will determine whether you use your challenging life experiences as opportunities for growth and recommitment to your vision for your life, or as a reason to simply give up on your hopes and dreams.

People who are happy don't necessarily have less adversity in their lives than others. They simply have learned that it's all about their self-talk. Everyone has preferences. We would prefer to keep our jobs (usually). We would prefer to be in good health. We would prefer to have the perfect family. But until those things occur, we must keep our eyes on the real goal, which is enjoyment of life right now. For example, I urged Sally to make a choice to rethink her situation and change her self-talk to go something like this: "I would prefer that my family members were loving to me and included me in their lives. But if I can't have that, my husband and I will start making new friends. We will create a new, healthy, more stable family—our "by choice' family." With this new, more positive self-talk, Sally came to feel a sense of control over her life and could look to the future with a far greater sense of optimism.

Unfortunately, quite a few of us succumb to the victim mindset that tells us, "He is making me unhappy," or "my age is making me unhappy," or "my job is making me unhappy." It's always some external factor—presumably outside our control—that makes us unhappy. But as you read this book, temporarily suspend all of your old beliefs about happiness and the conditions that are necessary for you to be happy ("I'll be happy when..."). Suspend the belief that your happiness—or lack of—is caused by something outside of yourself. Consider instead that your success in life and your happiness level is directly tied to your thoughts and the actions you take as a result of those thoughts.

THE INNER YOU

All of us have beliefs about why we function the way we do. My personal belief is that at the core of each of us is an Inner Being that is, at its essence, pure joy and wisdom. This Inner Being is what we sometimes call our soul or our spirit. It is always seeking happiness for you, and its mission—a simple one—is to provide the guidance that will lead you towards a joyous life—a gift for you and a gift for the universe. Your Inner Being is in direct contact with you through your emotions. When your thoughts, words, and actions are moving in a direction that will bring you joy, you experience positive emotions. When you have negative emotions, however, that means that your thoughts, words, and actions are taking you away from that which will bring you happiness.

Are you familiar with what we call "intuition"—those feelings in your gut that seem to be telling you that you should or shouldn't do something? That is your Inner Being (some call it your Soul) communicating with you through your feelings. Even though most of us don't communicate with our Inner Being through a dialogue of words, your Inner Being is still able to serve as a phenomenal guidance system using your emotions to alert you to what is going on. So, if you are feeling angry, anxious, or fearful, your Emotional Guidance System (EGS) is trying to tell you that what you are thinking, saying, or doing is taking you in the wrong direction and away from happiness. If, on the other hand, you are feeling content or even exhilarated, you know that you are acting in alignment with your Inner Being, and you are on a path to happiness.

WHERE DO YOU PLACE YOUR ATTENTION?

Whether you are thinking about the past, the present, or the future, what you feel right now is your life. In reality, all of us could experience more happiness in our lives—and very quickly—by simply shifting that to which we give our attention. When we pay more attention to the things that make us feel good, rather than the things that make us fearful, insecure or angry, we have the opportunity to experience joyous feelings on a continuous basis. If you focus on the good stuff, you feel good. If you focus on the bad stuff, you feel bad. It's that simple. Despite this "knowing," however, many of us still find value in utilizing supplemental strategies and exercises that will help us achieve a more fulfilling, satisfying life. It is to those of us who still seek our happiness the old fashioned way—we work for it—that the rest of this book is dedicated.

ACTION STEPS:

1. **Examine your beliefs about what it will take for you to be happy.** Ask yourself this question: "What is getting in the way of me taking responsibility for my happiness?" Does this statement below apply to you? "I believe that my circumstances have to change (lose weight, have a better job, make more money) before I can be happy." If your beliefs are getting in the way of your happiness, write down the beliefs that you can identify as standing in the way of being happy. (For example, "I need to lose 20 pounds before I can be happy.")

2. **Habitual behaviors can also get in the way of happiness such as**:
   I often complain about what is wrong in my life.
   I blame others or my circumstances for the difficulties in my life.
   I sometimes experience shame, believing that "It's all my fault."
   I focus more on what is negative in my life than what is positive.

   Write down any behaviors you can identify that sometimes get in the way of your happiness.

3. **Ask yourself, "Am I ready to take charge of my own happiness regardless of my circumstances. Am I ready to start identifying and eliminating beliefs and behaviors (complaining, blaming, shaming) that are interfering with happiness?"**

*The grace that happens is the emergence of the
beautiful human spirit, and the will toward well-being
and happiness despite the upheaval in one's life.*

CHAPTER 2

Finding Grace in Change

Some of the greatest challenges to our ability to be happy often come in the form of major life changes. Many of us have experienced life altering changes such as a job loss, the death of a spouse, a divorce, financial disaster or major health problems. In the blink of an eye, everything has changed. We have been forced to give up what we love, yet have no idea of how life will be after the change. When my husband first became ill and we realized that he would probably not recover, it felt like our world had crashed around us. We were afraid, we were angry, and we felt helpless. This man who had been active all of his life as a family physician and an ardent golfer was unable to walk, and found himself confined to a wheelchair with little motivation to leave the house. All of the fun things we had dreamed of doing in retirement—the golf, the parties, the traveling—seemed so out of reach. It all felt so unfair. How could this have happened to us? How were we going to regroup and rise above these things that were happening to us? How would we find the joy and the warm feelings that we had known before when we were mired in the sadness of our current situation?

Fortunately, I happened to recall a particularly inspiring book, written by Dr. Joan Borysenko entitled, *Saying Yes To Change.* In her book, Dr. Borysenko described a three-part rite of passage that author Joseph Campbell calls The Hero's Journey. The first part of the journey begins with the hero busily living life, often consumed with his own ambitions—perhaps getting that promotion, or impressing friends with a lifestyle that includes an enviable social status, an expensive sports car, or a house that is bigger and better than those of his or her friends—but often at the cost of spending less time with loved ones. In the second part of the journey, life suddenly and dramatically changes for the hero when an unalterable, profound event occurs that disrupts life as it used to be, and throws the hero into survival mode and onto an entirely new path with new challenges. The job is gone, the income is gone, the status is gone; the "toys" are gone. As the hero faces these challenges, he must give up his ego's desire to force its own will onto the situation. The emotions experienced by the hero are often similar to those Charles and I experienced—fear, anger, helplessness, and being in a kind of no-man's land with no idea how to cope—in fact, not wanting to have to deal with coping at all. In other words, we were hugely resistant to the unwanted change. For many, when the old life is a thing of the past, the entire focus is on the negativity of life in these new circumstances. With negativity as a focus, hopelessness and depression are never far behind. As well-intentioned friends sympathize with the plight of the hero, the feelings of self-pity quickly become pervasive, and the hero slides further into sadness and despair. The hero has no vision of the new life to come.

But then, as the hero (in our case, both Charles and me) begins to think about what is really important in life, insights start to occur. Breakthroughs happen, and a new approach to life is born. In the final transition to the third phase of the journey, the metamorphosis has occurred, and the hero has evolved into a wiser and more compassionate self. The grace that happens is the emergence of the beautiful human spirit, and the will toward well-being and happiness despite the upheaval in one's life. For Charles and me, in the words of my friend and mentor, Macky White, "we made the decision to spend the rest of our lives living, not dying." With this perspective, life becomes more precious, and loved ones become more treasured. What this means to you is that in your own personal times of crisis, as you find yourself having to give up the life you knew and loved, you can't necessarily rely on old beliefs— what you thought was important, your old ways of thinking and acting—to be in your best interest anymore. As Charles and I began to focus on the positive aspects of what we really wanted in our lives, it turned out that what emerged as the most important thing had nothing to do with what we were grieving over having lost (golf, trips, a fast-paced lifestyle.) For us, relationships—with each other, with our family, and with our friends—were at the top of our list of things that would bring us the fulfillment and life satisfaction that we wanted in whatever time we had left together. The grace that came with the dramatic change in our lives was learning the wisdom of accepting that which cannot be changed, focusing on things that uplifted us, and savoring the change that occurred deep within both of us. We knew clearly what we valued, and as we began living our values, we experienced the joy that comes with living in integrity with our values. Our thoughts, our words, and our actions were reflecting that which was most important to us. What a blessing that experience was. What grace. The danger for all of us when we are in crisis is that the stress of the situation has the potential to feel so great that anxiety, depression, and despondency can easily take over. But in these times of change, there is also an opportunity, and the opportunity is one of metamorphosis. Just as the caterpillar becomes encased in a chrysalis in which it actually liquefies before emerging as a graceful and beautiful butterfly, we, too, have to die to our old life. For only then can we make the transition from the person we were to the self of authentic wisdom, compassion, and true strength that comes in the third phase of The Hero's Journey.

In our four year journey during his illness, my husband and I may not have learned all the wisdom and eloquence of some who have made this journey, but we did learn some things that made our lives richer and more fulfilling as we traveled the road of change together. I have lost him, but I am determined that I won't lose the gift of grace—learning and honoring what really matters, and the softening of our hearts —that came with change. Perhaps you will find the suggestions that follow helpful as you travel your own path of change and experience the many opportunities for magical transformation that such a journey can bring to you and those who love you.

ACTION STEPS:

1. Recognize that you are always in transition. That is what life is all about.

2. Accept that while you may no longer feel a sense of control over your circumstances, you always have control over how you respond to your life circumstances.

3. Honor what was, but come to peace with life as it is. None of us like change, but coming to grips with impermanence and transition are key ingredients to true wisdom.

4. Make the shift from blaming others or God for your problems to accepting responsibility for creating a present that is different from your past.

5. Live in the moment with appreciation because all too quickly, the things you took for granted can suddenly be gone.

6. Understand that perhaps what happens "out there" isn't what life is all about. It is really what happens "in here" (your heart) as you find the grace to accept life on its own terms.

7. Find and nurture a new vision for the future.

8. Consider sharing the wisdom you gain along the way in your personal journey with others who may just be beginning theirs.

Why wait? Be happy now!

Charles and I found that our happiness depended,

in large part, on that upon which we chose to focus.

According to the Law of Attraction,

that to which you give your attention increases in your life.

So, if you spend your time giving your attention to how you only seem

to have bad luck, you may actually be attracting more bad luck.

CHAPTER 3

Achieving Happiness

WHAT MAKES YOU HAPPY?

As I talk with men and women of all ages, it is apparent to me that many people are struggling with their emotions. They describe feelings of worry, fear, disappointment and discouragement, and ask if there is a way to become happier. They want to feel a sense of contentment with life again. They want to feel hopeful and optimistic about the future. They want to experience joy and passion for what they are doing. Fortunately, research in the field of Positive Psychology by Martin Seligman, Ph.D., Sonja Lyubomirsky, Ph.D. and others has given us the information and some very promising tools to significantly improve our happiness level. There appear to be three factors that play the greatest role in determining how happy you are:

Your circumstances (whether you are rich or poor, healthy or unhealthy, good looking or unattractive, etc.) contribute to 10 percent of your happiness level.

Genetic makeup influences 50 percent of the variance in happiness levels. People appear to have a genetically determined set point for happiness similar to the set point for the weight you seem to most easily maintain. This set point represents your predisposition for happiness—how happy they are likely to be over the course of a lifetime.

Daily intentional activities are thought to influence the remaining 40 percent of your happiness level. This includes what you think and do in your daily life, such as monitoring your mindset, practicing gratitude, doing acts of kindness and many more activities you might choose.

The good news is that there is starting to be evidence that your set point for happiness, which is primarily influenced by your genetics and determines fifty percent of your happiness level, can be raised. It can be increased over time through the conscious choices you make about what you think and what you do in your daily intentional activities. One of my favorite examples of the power of well-chosen daily intentional activities came from a friend of mine named Jay. While serving in the military, Jay was stationed in an isolated area on a mountain in Japan. There was very little to do, and boredom and frustration were taking their toll on not only him, but the men who served under him as well. Jay noticed that some of the men, perhaps those with a lower set point for happiness, were feeling helpless and frustrated by their situation. In some cases, signs of depression were apparent. Jay's solution was to challenge each of his men to come up with a new idea each day for an activity that they would look forward to, and that would bring some pleasure to their otherwise dismal days. The men gradually began to get into the habit of creating activities that would promote positive feelings on a daily basis. Sometimes they would create games, such as their version of horseshoes. Sometimes they would take a group hike down the mountain and back up. Life became more pleasant, and not only did the men survive emotionally, they thrived. Through the daily intentional activities that these men consciously engaged in, they developed not only a higher level of happiness, but good will and friendships that would last a lifetime.

Given the proper understandings, information, tools and strategies, and some encouragement along the way to make life choices that will serve you well, you have everything it takes to make the choice to be happy now! It seems to me that research is soon going to conclude that Abraham Lincoln may have been right on the money when he said, "Most people are about as happy as they make up their minds to be."

THE LINE

In 1994 Dr. George Pransky and Dr. Roger Mills first introduced me to the idea that there is a line that separates those who are happy, fulfilled and successful in their lives from those who are unhappy, unfulfilled, and less successful at achieving their goals. In a workshop called Health Realization, they taught that fulfillment and happiness—even success—are determined by how people use their minds. What they focus on and how they think about events in their lives, all of which shape how they respond to those events, will determine whether they are functioning above the line: happy, successful, and enjoying life, or below the line: unhappy, unmotivated, and very low in energy.

Happiness

THE LINE

Unhappiness

A few years later, while attending a Harvard Medical School Clinical Training in Mind/Body Medicine, I studied key research findings on stress and its impact on our lives. One of the things we discussed was the fact that, when faced with stress and/or adversity, some people are inclined to feel helpless and give up, while others persevere toward their goals. So, the concept of "the line" was expanded to include above the line feelings of happiness, empowerment and a sense of being in control of your life, and below the line feelings of unhappiness, hopelessness, and feelings of helplessness and victimization. When facing adversity, empowered people focus on their strengths and the positive aspects of their situation. Those who take a victim stance focus on the negatives in their lives and their own sense of powerlessness, thus creating a very below the line existence for themselves, and a bleak outlook for future happiness.

Happiness ~ Empowerment ~ Sense of Control

THE LINE

Unhappiness ~ Helplessness ~ Hopeless Victim

One of my favorite examples of empowered thinking is the story told by Joan Borysenko, Ph.D. of several participants of a support group for women who had recently undergone mastectomies. Needless to say, the surgery had been extremely traumatic for most of the women, and they had very different emotional responses. One woman who felt helpless and was definitely functioning below the line said, "My whole life is ruined. I'm so ugly that nobody will ever love me again." This woman became more and more unhappy and lacking in self-confidence, eventually isolating herself completely from the people in her life she cared most about. In contrast, another woman in the group dramatically empowered herself and her ability to remain above the line with her attitude, "I may not be perfect, but parts of me are excellent, and I intend to get back into life full speed ahead!" But how can we feel happy and enthusiastic when our lives seem to be falling apart, and we feel like we don't have any control over anything that is happening to us? Finding happiness in these circumstances can be daunting, but the starting point is always remembering that how you use your mind—your thinking—is going to play a major role in your ability to rise above adversity. What you tell yourself in tough situations will not only determine how you feel about the situation, it will determine how you respond. If you tell yourself, "I can handle this. Everything will be okay," you are more likely to be able to keep your spirits up, and stay motivated toward finding a solution, than if you don't believe in your ability to rise above whatever is going on. If, however, you tell yourself, "My life is ruined. I'll never be happy again. I might as well just give up," you are experiencing the attitude of a pessimist who never feels a sense of control over his or her life, and definitely experiences very little happiness and life satisfaction. It seems as if the cause of your miserable feelings is "out there" and there is no way you can feel better until "out there" changes. Research and wisdom traditions of the past, however, all point us to a very different viewpoint. They point us to the understanding that it's not "out there" that has to change.

It is what we are telling ourselves about our circumstances and what we do in response to our self-talk (the actions we take) that determine how happy or unhappy we are going to be. One of Charles' sayings that ranked among my favorites was, "Don't tell me why it can't be done. Tell me how it can be done." This was the self-talk, this was the spirit, this was the pervasive attitude that kept us trying, kept us engaged in life, and kept us enjoying the time we had left together. This was the self-talk that shaped our daily intentional activities. "Out there" wasn't going to change for us. Any changes that occurred had to come from within us.

DO YOU FOCUS ON THE GARDENS OR THE DUMPS?

Charles and I found that our happiness depended, in large part, on that upon which we chose to focus. According to the Law of Attraction, that to which you give your attention increases in your life. So, if you spend your time giving your attention to how you only seem to have bad luck, you may actually be attracting more bad luck. Such a focus keeps your emotions at a very low level, as well as your ability to take constructive action. Things just seem to keep getting worse and worse.

The following example about the gardens and the dumps kept me reminded that what I focus on is always my choice, and will ultimately determine how much I enjoy any aspect of my life. Imagine that you just moved to a new community, and you discovered many beautiful gardens as you drove through town. There was, however, one small location that contained the town dump. Needless to say, there was very little about the town dump that was attractive. In fact, it was disgusting! Here is the key question: In determining how you

29

feel about the town, are you going to focus on the town's beautiful gardens which are all around you, or are you going to give your attention to the town dump?" If you choose to focus on the gardens, your experience in the community will be a very pleasant one. If, however, you decide to focus on the dump—the uglier, less desirable aspect of the town—you will find that you experience very little enjoyment in the community. When you are going through any challenge in your life, what you focus on is always a choice, and that choice will determine whether you experience the gardens or the dumps of life—and the feelings that go with it.

If you found yourself wondering, "Why would anyone focus on the town dump when they could focus on the beautiful gardens," you may also be asking the question, "Why would anyone choose to function below the line when they could be functioning above the line?" The answer is that we usually don't realize what we are doing. We forget that our emotions are caused by our thoughts, not by our circumstances. Remember, how you feel about anything is always directly connected to what you are thinking about your situation—what aspects of the situation you are giving your attention to. If you are experiencing a great deal of frustration, discouragement, anger—even feelings of hopelessness and despair—you want to check on two things:

1. What am I telling myself about the situation?

2. Where is my focus? Am I giving my attention to the gardens or the dumps in this situation?

When your self-talk about your circumstances results in emotions like contentment, hope, even enthusiasm, you are on the right track with your self-talk. And, even if you are struggling with your self-talk, you can choose to focus in on things that are enjoyable, things that provide you with hope, pleasure and optimism including your friends, a beautiful day, a lovely home—the pleasures of the moment. You soon begin to feel more empowered to manage your life. You begin to think more clearly. Your interactions with other people are better, and life tends to feel much more positive—all because of the choices you are making. Below is a brief version of the story about the Wise Old Man that most of us have seen several times on the internet. It is the classic lesson in how a person's attitude—what that person chooses to focus on—can make all the difference between happiness and unhappiness.

> A man of 92 years is moving into a senior living facility today. His wife has died, and he has determined that this move is the appropriate one for him. After waiting quite a long time in the lobby, he gently smiles as he is told that his room is ready. As he slowly walks to the elevator using his cane, the staff person describes his room to him. "I like it very much," he says enthusiastically. Surprised, the staff person said, "Sir, you haven't even seen the room yet." "That has nothing to do with it," he replies. "Happiness is something I choose in advance. Whether or not I like the room doesn't depend on the décor. Rather, it depends on how I decide to see it. It is already decided in my mind that I like my room. I make these decisions every morning when I wake up. I can choose. For example, I can spend my day in bed enumerating all the difficulties that I have with the parts of my body that no longer work very well, or I can get up and give thanks to heaven for those parts that are still in working order."

Happiness is a choice you make. It is a perspective you choose each day. What you think about—what you focus on—the story you tell yourself in any situation—will always be key factors in the amount of joy and happiness you experience in your life. Your feelings will always be directly linked to your thoughts, beliefs, and what you tell yourself about whatever circumstances you are currently experiencing. These concepts form the basic foundation for happiness. The next step is to equip yourself with additional strategies found throughout this book that will enhance your resilience, your self-esteem, and the extent to which you are able to raise your happiness set point, and increase the amount of happiness you experience in your life.

ACTION STEPS:

1. The next time you are faced with a challenging situation, ask yourself if there is anything you can do to remedy the situation. If the answer is yes, take action. If you cannot change your circumstances, go to Action Step #2.

2. If you cannot change your situation, ask yourself, "What am I telling myself about this situation? Is my self-talk discouraging me, and keeping me from engaging in activities that would help me get through this?" If your answer is "yes." Go to Action Step #3.

3. Consider how you might change (reframe) what you are telling yourself about your situation, so that you will feel more energized and ready to jump back into life. (Keep in mind the woman who, after a mastectomy, took the approach, "I may not be perfect, but parts of me are excellent, and I intend to get back into life full speed ahead.")

4. If you are having trouble finding more positive self-talk, keep in mind the contribution of daily intentional activities, which will be discussed more fully in Part II. Try distracting from your concerns by engaging in some activities that bring you pleasure, such as sports, or doing kind things for others, feeling appreciation for the good things in your life. Sometimes it really is the small stuff that makes the difference!

Why wait? Be happy now!

If you are experiencing doubt, worry, blame or any of the negative emotions, you are probably giving yourself some pretty negative messages about your life or your situation, and those negative messages are showing up as negative emotions.

CHAPTER 4

What Role Do My Emotions Play?

One might say that people are either happy or unhappy. Or that we either have good feelings or bad feelings. In their book, *Ask and It Is Given*, Jerry and Esther Hicks have clarified that in between happiness/empowerment and unhappiness/helplessness, there is a range of emotions that you might be experiencing at any given time.

All of us are somewhere on this scale all of the time. Many people either believe that where they are on the emotional scale at any given time just happens by accident or that it is due to their circumstances. Do you ever finding yourself saying, "I wonder why I'm in such a good mood today? Or "I wonder why I'm so crabby today?" In reality, if you are experiencing doubt, worry, blame or any of the negative emotions, you are probably giving yourself some pretty negative messages about your life or your situation, and those negative messages are showing up as negative emotions.

Happiness Scale

Unconditional Happiness
Passion, Joy, Love of Life
Enthusiasm, Eagerness
Positive Expectations, Optimism
Hopefulness, Compassion
Contentment

THE LINE

Pessimism, Frustration
Discouragement, Overwhelment, Disappointment
Doubt, Worry
Guilt, Blame, Anger, Fear,
Unhappiness, Despair, Helplessness, Hopelessness

Where you are on the scale at any given time can make all the difference in what kind of a day you have, ranging from delightful and extremely enjoyable to dismal. Where you are also makes a difference in how you interact with the world. You respond differently from a place of compassion and/or positive expectations than from a place of frustration, worry, anger, or fear.

Where you fall on this continuum will be impacted by the three things we talked about in Chapter Three:

1. Your genetic set point (50%)

2. Your circumstances (10%)

3. How you use your thinking, and the activities you choose to engage in (40%)

Let's say that your genetic happiness set point places you somewhere around the doubt and worry level. Let's also say that you have just lost your job, so your circumstances pull you down toward anger and fear. But your goal is to be above the line somewhere in the happiness feelings. You have no control over your circumstances, so your thinking may go something like this: "There may be nothing I can do about my job circumstances right now, but I am going to spend a lot of quality time with my family, while I am deciding on how I will get my career back on track." Your focus, then, becomes seeking and engaging in fun, inexpensive family activities, which might be as simple as gathering together in the living room to share the best things about each person's week so far. Sometimes this is exactly the kind of quality family interaction that you haven't had for years! There is a very good chance that, at a minimum, you will find yourself experiencing the positive emotion of contentment.

EMOTIONAL GUIDANCE SYSTEM

I like to think of the various levels of emotions up and down the Happiness Scale as my personal Emotional Guidance System. When I set goals in my life, such as the goal of warm relationships with family and friends, or living in integrity with my values, my emotions always let me know whether I am on the right track and moving toward my goal, or on the wrong track and moving away from my goal. It works just like the navigational system in your car. You can plug in your destination (your goal), and your feelings tell you whether you are headed in the right direction. Let's say you have a goal of harmony in your relationships. But you have just had an argument with a friend who said something hateful to you. You may be experiencing feelings of anger, and want to respond with some hateful remarks of your own—quite the opposite of your destination of harmonious relationships. Your feelings of anger are your guidance system's alarm that you are off track from your stated destination, and that you need to step back from the situation and gain some perspective. As Stephen Covey would say, "begin with the end in mind." The "end in mind" is a harmonious relationship. Thus, your new perspective might be one of compassion for your friend, whom you know has just divorced her husband, is trying to raise three children by herself, and is also experiencing significant financial difficulties. As you change what you are thinking, you are likely to find that you are once again enjoying the above the line feelings of warmth and compassion. While you may need to tell your friend that it is not okay to talk to you as she did, you are likely to find that your anger, and the harsh words that accompany that anger, have mellowed significantly, and you are once again enjoying the "above-the-line" happiness emotions.

My personal belief is that all of us are innately happy. If you observe children, you will notice that by and large, their default setting seems to be one of enjoying life. We just sometimes lose track of that happiness along the way. Therefore, the primary destination that we want to plug into our Emotional

Guidance System to get ourselves back on track is Happiness. Your emotions then work like any other GPS in that they provide you the best route to your own personal happiness. When you are experiencing contentment, peace, optimism, and enthusiasm, you know your thoughts, words, and actions are moving you toward your goal of happiness. If, instead, you are experiencing pessimism, frustration, disappointment, fear or anger, you know you have deviated from your route to happiness. Specifically, your thoughts, your words and your actions (all of which generate your emotions) are taking you in the wrong direction. Can't you just hear that your guidance system is saying, "Alert! Alert! Please make a U-turn and return to the highlighted route (your path to happiness)." When your EGS (Emotional Guidance System) is on high alert, and your emotions are screaming at you to pay attention, you need to examine your thoughts (which give impetus to your words and actions) to discover the source of negativity. Then, work on consciously shifting your thinking and actions to better align with your goal of happiness.

CHECK IT OUT

Your awareness of your emotions, and ability to take action to change direction if you are off track, are essential to staying above the line in the range of happy (positive) emotions. Take a moment to ask yourself these questions:

1. Do I see my emotions as something I have some control over?

2. Do I quickly recognize and acknowledge when I am experiencing negative emotions?

3. Do I assess the situation objectively, and look for indicators of unwarranted negative thinking that is pulling me "below the line?"

4. Do I easily identify thinking that is working against my best interests such as "She was so hateful to me. If that is the way she is going to be, I can be that way too."

5. Do I recognize my Emotional Guidance System's warning bells, and make the necessary adjustments? For example, you might shift your thinking to, "She really does have a lot of problems in her life right now. I can certainly be the one to take the first steps toward mending our relationship."

IT'S WHAT WE TELL OURSELVES THAT MATTERS!

So back to basics. Whenever you want to raise your happiness level, you don't need to go outside of yourself. You don't need to win the lottery. You don't need a boyfriend You don't need to spend $300 on new cosmetics. In short, you don't need to change your circumstances. You simply need to check out two things:

1. Notice what is happening and how you feel. If you are experiencing below the line feelings, ask yourself, "What am I telling myself that is pulling me down emotionally?

2. Since you are wanting to make the shift to better feeling thoughts that produce better feelings, ask yourself:

"Do I need to think about my situation in a more positive light?

Or, do I need to take my attention completely off this situation that is pulling me down, and instead, focus on thoughts and activities that tend to make me feel good?"

You always have a choice what you are going to tell yourself about any situation. You have a choice about what you are going to focus on, and what you are going to do. The choices you make will determine whether you are enjoying one of the emotions above the line such as contentment, optimism, or joy, or putting up with the less pleasant emotions below the line such as frustration, doubt, worry and fear. I live it, I teach it; it works! For four years Charles and I dealt with his horrendous health situation, including the amputation of his right let, and his inability to ambulate without a wheelchair. He was unable to play golf (his lifelong retirement dream), and I had to give up a career that I loved along with much of my social life. We could each have spent those years angry, frustrated, and disappointed about what we both had given up, and worried about what each new day would bring health-wise. The other choice was to keep our thoughts focused on the good stuff, and find things to do that we enjoyed. Because we were committed to making whatever time we had left together quality time (happiness for ourselves and those around us), we made a very conscious choice to keep our minds focused on the positive things. These included a deepening of our emotional intimacy, the intentional enjoyment of the small stuff, and giving thanks for each day we were given. We were constantly teaching each other how to pull ourselves up when we were discouraged, and avoid wallowing in the self-pity that could have so easily consumed us. By supporting one another, and intentionally using the strategies that you will find throughout this book, we were able to keep our emotions above the line almost all of the time. I will admit that every once in a while, we would just give ourselves permission to cry, and that's okay too. Tears can sometimes be very therapeutic.

IT'S NICER ABOVE THE LINE

As you can imagine, life is a lot nicer and a lot more enjoyable when you live above the line. The way you think about things and the way you feel is considerably different — more optimistic, more positive, more motivating, more conducive to success—from above the line than from below the line. And the best part about learning to live above the line is that, once you get the hang of this, you don't need to keep reading books about how to be happy. You will become the expert! You will rarely have to ask, "What am I supposed to do when this happens?" because you will know what to do to increase your happiness level and make you feel better. All you have to do is pay attention, and make adjustments from time to time.

ACTION STEPS:

1. The next time you notice below the line emotions, such as disappointment, doubt, worry, blame, anger or fear, praise yourself for tuning in to your Emotional Guidance System's warning bells.

2. Remember to (a) take action if you can to change your situation, (b) examine what you are telling yourself about your situation and try to change your self-talk if it is pulling you down, and (c) when you can't change your circumstances, use other intentional activities to distract from your situation and give you additional pleasure in your life.

3. Keep your eye on the ball. Your goal is to gradually increase your happiness level—the amount of time you spend in pleasant feelings. You may not make huge gains initially, but you will gradually develop your "happiness muscle," and even just a little additional time spent in good feelings is a win!

Why wait? Be happy now!

While it is important to recognize the reality of your adverse situation, you are far more likely to overcome difficulties in your life and remain happy if you develop the ability to work your way up to a more constructive, more optimistic way of thinking about the challenges you are facing.

CHAPTER 5

How Can I Be Happy When My World is Falling Apart?

When things are going well in our lives, most of us find it fairly easy to stay above the line, at least at the level of contentment. The real challenge to your happiness comes when major problems occur in your life such as the loss of a job, health problems, or in my case, the loss of a loved one. Researchers have found that feelings of happiness and feelings of empowerment are closely linked. Have you ever noticed that you are far more likely to maintain your feelings of well-being when you feel that you have some power over your life. Such power is usually felt when you have confidence in your ability to handle whatever challenges come your way. Researchers call this kind of confidence "self-efficacy." Helplessness, unhappiness, and even despair, on the other hand, are often experienced when you feel that you have no control over your circumstances or your happiness. You believe that any action on your part would make very little difference. You feel powerless. You feel victimized. You have little motivation to continue your efforts to improve your situation, and you are likely to begin showing signs of depression. The difference between feeling empowered and feeling helpless is usually the major reason why some people enjoy life and keep pursuing their goals with enthusiasm at any age, while others become discouraged and basically disengage from life. Feelings of empowerment move you up on the happiness scale, and you tend to be more engaged with life. Feelings of helplessness, on the other hand, and lack of confidence in your ability to handle challenges that come your way, will drain your energy, lower your spirits, and diminish the likelihood that you will live a full and satisfying life. The feelings experienced during a typical day for someone with a sense of empowerment can be very different from the feelings of someone who has low self-esteem and does not feel empowered. For example, when I feel empowered, I feel optimistic. I don't question my self worth. My sense of self-efficacy is strong, and I know I am capable and effective. I wake up in the morning looking forward to a nice day. When I'm working, I'm highly motivated, organized and efficient. I'm able to prioritize my tasks for the day and complete them with plenty of energy left to enjoy friends and family. When I don't feel empowered, and my self-confidence is low, I tend to be more pessimistic and lower in energy, partly from worrying during the night about yesterday's problems, or what might happen tomorrow. I am more irritable, and more likely to "nit-pick" the people I am with. I sometimes have trouble starting projects because I don't feel my usual sense of confidence and competence. I tend to alienate friends and family. Even my dog avoids me.

EMPOWERMENT IS A GREAT CONTRIBUTOR TO HAPPINESS

One of the greatest contributors to happiness is a sense of empowerment. Researchers Suzanne Oulette, Ph.D. (her name was Kobasa when the original work was published) and her colleagues, including Dr. Salvadore Maddi, studied business executives undergoing the stress of their company's divestiture. They found that there are some very specific characteristics found in the mindsets of people who are stress-hardy, or resilient. These characteristics are a sense of **control** over one's life, viewing adversity as a

challenge, and a sense of **commitment** to whatever you undertake (a sense of purpose). Hardiness, also known as resilience, is defined as the ability to deal well with stress, and bounce back from adversity, and is directly correlated with physical and mental health and wellbeing.

Control: When faced with adversity, the empowered person says, "I might not be able to control my circumstances, but I certainly can control the attitude I bring to this situation." Control is a belief that you can positively influence the outcome of an adverse event instead of becoming a victim to it. When you have a sense of control over your life, you recognize that while you might not be able to choose the circumstances in which you find yourself, you can definitely choose how you respond to those circumstances. You generally have the belief that you can cushion the hurtful impact of a situation by the way you look at it and respond to it. Control, in this context, is not the erroneous belief that you can control your environment, your circumstances, or other people. It is the healthy belief that you can control yourself, and your own reactions to what life hands you.

Challenge: The empowered person says, "This is a difficult challenge, but I know I can handle it and maintain my sense of well being." The helpless person says, "This is a catastrophe. I'll never be happy again." Challenge means the ability to see change and/or adversity as an opportunity for growth and improvement rather than as something threatening or catastrophic. A stress-hardy (resilient) person faces change with confidence, self-determination, eagerness and excitement. Change becomes an eagerly sought-after challenge, not a threat. A person who is not resilient views change with helplessness and alienation. According to Oullette, the key to hardiness and wellness is a different way of looking at and dealing with stress and adversity.

Commitment: The empowered person says, "I am committed to staying as happy as I possibly can, and to doing whatever it takes to improve this situation." Commitment is an attitude of involvement in what is happening around you. It means a commitment to yourself, your work, your family, and other important values in your life. People who are committed have a deep sense of meaning and purpose, and a pervasive sense of direction in their lives.

EMPOWERMENT DOESN'T HAPPEN BY ACCIDENT

The landmark works of many top researchers such as Martin Seligman, author of the book, *Authentic Happiness,* make it clear that managing stress and adversity well and finding happiness don't happen by accident. People who are happy and successful are not necessarily born lucky. They just know what they want and have an understanding of how to get it. They know what makes them happy and they have the necessary mindset and skills to respond effectively when the going gets tough. Happiness isn't out there somewhere waiting to be found. Happiness is right here all the time just waiting for you to bring it forth. It has been my experience that the happiest people use some very specific strategies that allow them to respond effectively to whatever adversity is occurring in their lives. For example, although Charles and I certainly had very little control over our situation, we certainly had control over how we approached each day. We didn't wake up each day wondering what the day would bring. We woke up planning what we would bring to the day. We considered every day as a challenge, and our job was to make each day as enjoyable as possible. We were committed to happiness, always knowing that we had a choice about how we were going to respond to each new problem that came our way. And when the inevitable problems did arise, our goal was always to choose happiness—staying above the line. In today's environment of change and uncertainty, it is more important than ever to have a stash of skills and strategies that you can use to bounce back as you come up against the difficult situations that life throws your way.

It is important to deeply understand—to really "get it in your bones"—that the characteristics of hardiness or resilience mentioned above are essential to your ability to remain motivated, to persevere in difficult times, and to keep happiness as your focus. Even more important is the knowledge that even if you don't have these characteristics well developed now, these characteristics can be learned. You will feel more empowered and more confident as you develop your personalized philosophies of living that work for you, a mindset that promotes resilience and becomes the basis of your self-talk, and certain strategies by which hardiness and resilience to stress and adversity can be achieved.

It takes time and a strong commitment to change beliefs and old ways of responding and doing things. It is easier to make changes and become more effective, more successful and happier in your life when you have a clear path to follow that will lead you to the achievement of your goals and desires. The strategies presented in the following chapters are the ones that we found we needed to stay above the line and maintain a sense of well-being during Charles illness. They are grounded in research on resilience and happiness, and are combined with many practical tools for overcoming adversity and achieving the fulfillment and happiness you want in your life. These strategies include:

- Living consciously (knowing who you are and loving it!)

- Having a clear vision for your life as you want it to be.

- Cultivating a bounce-back, above the line attitude that is essential for resilience and happiness.

- Developing life skills that strengthen your ability to live life as you want it to be.

- Maintaining a lifestyle of self-care that allows you to fully enjoy the life you are creating for yourself, regardless of your circumstances. In the end, success is not measured by the money you make or the stuff you gather. Success is measured by the amount of joy you experience during your journey through life. In short, life is supposed to be fun!

ACTION STEPS:

1. The next time you are faced with a challenging situation, ask yourself these questions about the 3 Cs of empowerment:

   Am I looking at this problem as a personal **challenge** or as a catastrophe? Can I see this as an opportunity for growth?

   Am I **committed** to my goal of staying above the line as I work through this?

   Am I retaining a sense of **control** by either taking steps to change the situation, or by changing the attitude that I bring to the situation?

The difference between feeling empowered and feeling helpless is usually the major reason why some people enjoy life and keep pursuing their goals with enthusiasm at any age, while others become discouraged and basically disengage from life.

CHAPTER 6
What Do You Mean I Missed My Exit?
(LIVING CONSCIOUSLY)

If you were to take only one understanding from this book, this is what I hope you would take: You are an amazingly powerful person. You have the power to create your life as you want it to be. The source of your ability to create is your thoughts—what you wish for, what you tell yourself about things that happen to you and your clarity about things you want and don't want in your life.

Sometimes, however, it is easy to forget just how powerful you are. Rather than carefully choosing the thoughts that will contribute to the creation of a happy, productive life, it is so easy to become "unconscious."

Did you ever have the experience of driving along an interstate highway, and all of the sudden you have no awareness of whether or not you passed your exit? I certainly have! Once I missed my exit by thirty miles because my mind was way off somewhere else. I was driving unconsciously!

Many of us live our lives that way. Life just breezes right by us. Good things happen, bad things happen, and we are just getting those good and bad things by default—not by our deliberate intention. We aren't planning or creating them. They just seem to happen. It rarely occurs to us that, "Hey, I want some input into what kind of life I'm creating here—and we are creating it whether we realize it or not. You are attracting things and people into your life through the power of your thought. It's all about what you focus on. The thoughts in your head determine how you feel, what you say, what you do—and ultimately, what you experience in life.

The first step toward "being happy now" is to live consciously. Living consciously means living your life with great awareness, consciously making choices about what you want in life, what you value in life, the goals you will strive for, and how you will respond to circumstances and other people in your life.

WHO ARE YOU AND WHAT DO YOU WANT?

There is a wonderful story about the philosopher, Peter Russell, who had this message on his telephone answering machine:

"Who are you and what do you want? If you think these are frivolous questions they are not. Most people come into this world and leave it again without having answered either one."

The art of "being happy now" involves living with great awareness. It involves thinking through who you are, what you want, building any skills you need such as challenging old, limiting beliefs, and then setting off on your path to create a richer, fuller, more satisfying life for yourself.

Living consciously means making choices about what you value in life, the goals you will strive for, and understanding that it is truly you that will create your life—and not your circumstances or other people. It always has been so.

CHOOSING OUTCOMES.

Our lives are made up of many facets including:

Health	Relationships	Career
Wealth	Family	Use of leisure time

Living consciously means carefully choosing what you want these areas and other aspects of your life to look like. Take the time to consciously reflect on each area and get very clear about exactly what you are wanting from your life in this area. For example, if you are reflecting on health, you might want to say to yourself, "I see myself growing healthier every day. I see myself eating nutritious foods and exercising in a way that will help me achieve my desired weight and my goal of good health." The clearer you are in your mind about what you desire in each of these areas, the more your thoughts, words, and actions will bring you toward the outcomes you want.

In order to bring greater clarity to the outcomes I want in each of these key areas, I sit quietly for twenty minutes each day and consciously give thought to exactly what I want in the various aspects of my life. Since beginning this practice, my life has seemed to come together effortlessly. I am clearer about the words I choose in conversations with others, and my actions are congruent with my thoughts, values and beliefs. Each day's activities seem to bring me closer to the outcomes I desire in each of these areas.

Living consciously also means getting rid of what you don't want.

It is so easy to go through life making mechanical responses to situations. You don't really think about your response. You simply react based on old habits, old beliefs, conditioning from other people, and old ways of doing things that may no longer be serving you well. As a simple example, my husband and I almost always had a TV blaring every newsworthy item that had occurred anywhere in the world. Much of it was depressing, and tended to really lower my spirits, as well as my hope for the world. More recently, I have made the choice not to have the TV turned on so frequently. I watch a brief news summary at noon and on the six o'clock news, and that is about it. I've noticed that I spend considerably less time worrying about the stock market, or which country we will be at war with next. The only downside is that I occasionally miss a really good story about acts of kindness, but, unfortunately, those don't seem to make the news all that often these days.

DO YOU REACT OR DO YOU RESPOND?

It is so easy to go through life making mechanical responses to situations, simply reacting to people and events based on old habits, old beliefs, destructive and/or limiting self-talk, and old ways of doing things that may no longer be serving you well. In that situation, you don't consciously think about your responses. You just react.

It is a wiser choice, albeit a more challenging choice (but oh so rewarding), to be proactive by consciously giving thought to life as you want it to be and how you want to respond to people and events in your life based on your values, goals, and a belief system that you have weighed carefully. You don't have to respond based on old habits.

For example, if you lost your job, your old habitual belief might be, "People who don't work are bums. I'm without a job, so I must be a bum." Needless to say, when you hold such a belief, your self-esteem plummets, along with your belief that you can alter the situation. A more helpful response or belief might be, "I may be out of work now, but I know my skills are good, and my attitude is excellent. I will actively look for another job, and while I'm doing that, I'm going to enjoy some long overdue time with my family."

CHOOSE YOUR THOUGHTS. LET YOUR FEELINGS BE YOUR GUIDE.

Since you are reading this book, it is probably a fair assumption that you want more happiness in your life. By now you know that if you want to be happy, the best practice, while difficult at times, is to direct your thoughts toward things that stimulate the feelings you are looking for, such as hope, optimism, and appreciation for that which is good in your life.

What isn't always so simple, however, is living with enough awareness to monitor your thoughts. It is much easier to monitor your feelings. When you realize that you are experiencing below the line feelings (sadness, anger, frustration), bring your awareness to the thoughts that are producing the undesirable feelings. For example, were you thinking, "I'm without a job, so I must be a bum."

Once you have identified the thinking that resulted in unpleasant feelings, you can then choose to redirect your thoughts to something that will shift you into a better place, such as, "While I'm looking for a new job, I'll have more time to enjoy my family." Placing your attention on something more pleasant can distract you from unwanted thoughts and feelings, lift your spirits, and renew your energy.

CHOOSE YOUR ATTITUDE

Just as you might consciously choose your friends or the kind of work you enjoy doing, it is also important to consciously choose your attitudes and beliefs about your life. For example, some people deal with situations such as a job loss by blaming others. Some people blame themselves. Some choose to see the glass half full. Others choose to see the glass half empty. Some believe they can achieve anything they set their mind too. Others listen to old tapes of negativity playing in their head that say, "No one in our family has ever gone to college. Education is a waste of money. You don't need more education to take over the family business," or "No one in our family has ever become a writer. You're wasting your time," or "Everyone in our family is heavy. No need trying all that weight loss stuff," or "My mother and grandmother died in their early seventies. There's not much point in me eating all that health food and exercising so much. I'll probably be just like them."

Some people choose to live with anger and resentment when others don't treat them as they would like. They hang on to their anger like a hot coal. Others, who realize that the only one burned by the hot coal of their anger is them, will choose to let go of anger and resentment, and choose peace instead.

You can often tell which attitudes and beliefs are constructive and helpful by the way they make you feel. When you are telling yourself that, "the rest of our family died young, so I probably will too," the chances are pretty good that you aren't energized or motivated to take care of yourself, get the proper nutrition, and exercise on a regular basis. On the other hand, your self-talk may be more like, "My mother and grandmother may have died relatively young, but times have changed. People today are taking better care of themselves and they are living longer, healthier, happier, and more fulfilled lifestyles than were available back then. I'm healthy now and I'm going to do everything in my power to stay that way." If that is the case, you are probably choosing your food wisely, finding ways to get the right amount of exercise, and well on your way to a healthy, enjoyable life.

"THAT'S JUST THE WAY I AM!"

One type of conscious choice we have is the choice of how we are going to respond to people who press our hot-buttons. When talking with clients, I sometimes hear them say things like, "My family members have always been hot tempered. That's just the way we are," or "I get angry at the drop of a hat. That's just the way I am!" These people don't realize that they have control over their emotions and their responses. In fact, they sometimes even reject the idea that they might be able to change by taking responsibility for their attitudes, emotions, and responses.

Openness to changing your perspective, and a willingness to hold yourself accountable for making needed changes are essential for living with awareness, for sustaining happiness, for improving your resilience, and for moving you toward successful achievement of your goals and dreams. A good starting point to this kind of openness is to try to avoid falling victim to the "that's just the way I am" mentality.

CHOOSING HOW YOU RESPOND

The ability to consciously think about how you are going to respond to challenges that come your way, weigh alternatives, and choose the most effective response is a defining characteristic of human beings. When someone says something upsetting, we sometimes use this ability to give thought to our responses, and sometimes we just thoughtlessly react. When you don't give conscious thought to how you want to respond, the process looks like this:

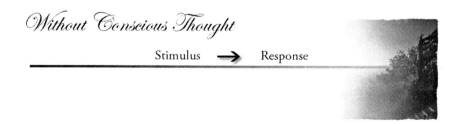

Without Conscious Thought

Stimulus ➔ Response

There is no thought. No weighing of alternatives, no conscious choice based on which of the responses available to you would be most effective in achieving the outcome you desire. Life is happening to you by default, and that approach may not be serving you well.

However, when you use your ability to weigh the situation and choose what you believe to be the most effective response, and one that is most consistent with your values and your goals for your life, the process looks like this:

With Conscious Thought

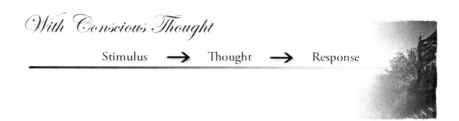

Stimulus   →   Thought   →   Response

Because so many of our responses or reactions were learned in childhood, it is easy to fall back on habitual ways of doing things. In my family, when I did something that upset my mother, she would walk off in a huff, hoping that by punishing me in this way, I would "come around" to her way of thinking. I never did like how that strategy made me feel as a child. However, as an adult, to my dismay, I discovered that I was reacting in this same way (leaving the room in a huff) when my children did something I didn't like.

Like my mother, I walked off in a huff, hoping for an apology and/or change in behavior from my children. To my knowledge, walking off in a huff wasn't an effective response by my mother when I was a child, nor was it effective with my children. It was simply a conditioned response that I learned early in childhood. Conflict was the stimulus, walking off in a huff was the conditioned response or reaction. I had never stopped to consider that I could choose a different response—one that had a much better feeling to it and would have been more effective as well.

Fortunately, I finally learned that it is far more productive (even if sometimes more painful) to stick around and try to calmly and earnestly talk through the problem rather than to walk away. That response is now my choice, and the choice I encourage for my coaching clients as well.

I was recently working with a couple, Steve and Sarah, who had been married for ten years. They seemed to be very much in love and totally dedicated to their own and each other's happiness. However, they had one major stumbling block in their relationship (a second marriage for both). Steve had a son by his first marriage who had abused alcohol and other drugs since he was in middle school. He is now 38 years old, continues to abuse drugs, and has been unable to support himself or sustain success in his business and financial life. When he gets in financial straits, which is quite often, he calls and his father bails him out. Sarah is becoming fearful, and quite anxious around the subject of money. She fears that the financial security they have enjoyed to this point, but which was greatly damaged when the stock market drastically declined, is going to be a thing of the past. Steve, who lost his other child in infancy, understands the "tough love" approach that many have recommended, but feels a strong need to continue rescuing his son. His typical pattern is to become quite defensive when Sarah tries to discuss her concerns.

During a joint coaching session, both Steve and Sarah talked about their concerns, and the more they talked, the more Sarah dug in her heels around her position of fear that their money would be depleted by the son who refuses to take responsibility for his own life. Her anger toward the son escalated to the point where she told Steve that she wants the son out of her life, even though she knows he will continue to be a part of Steve's life.

During moments of extreme frustration as we discussed the multifaceted issues around this situation, Sarah almost walked out in anger. Fortunately, Sarah had learned that such a response would do nothing to improve their situation, and she chose to remain and continue trying to find ways of dealing with the problem that would be acceptable to both Sarah and Steve. While we weren't able to find answers to all of the problems during that session, both Sarah and Steve refocused on the outcome they want (keeping love and joy in their marriage), and they were able to return their feeling state to love for one another by the time we concluded. In other words, rather than just reacting to the painful stimulation (their respective stances regarding the son), they were able to rise above it and take a wiser approach, one that restored trust and willingness to work together on some strategies that we laid out together.

CATASTROPHIC EVENTS

Often catastrophic events, such as those which occurred on September 11, 2001, greatly increase our recognition of the importance of living our lives with awareness and conscious choice making. In the midst of chaos, we often find ourselves looking critically at and challenging old beliefs that have shaped our choices and our actions for years. Sometimes we are faced with accepting the fact that our old ways of doing things and some of our old beliefs may no longer be serving us well. For example, many people have believed that it didn't matter how many hours they worked, and how little time they spent with their family, as long as they were "successful" and making enough money to buy all the "toys" they wanted. In crisis, however, they are likely to reprioritize and make conscious choices about changes in their careers and personal lives. Sometimes crisis reminds us to spend less time working, and reinvest in relationships by deepening our commitment to those we care about. We may consciously choose to recommit to our vision for our lives and to the success of a career we love. In essence, it is all about awareness and choices.

WHAT DO YOU BELIEVE TO BE TRUE ABOUT LIFE?

Living consciously means knowing what you believe to be true about life. I received an email that included a poem by Donna Maris. Her poem provides a very nice summary of many of my key beliefs about life. She calls her poem, *A Life Well Lived*. The poem makes the point that when I die, it won't matter what I owned. It won't matter whether I was wealthy. It won't matter if I was clever, beautiful, or brilliant. What will matter—what will be the measure of my life—is not what I have received, but what I have shared; not what I have learned, but what I have taught. What will matter is caring acts of integrity, compassion, courage or sacrifice that enriched, empowered, or encouraged others. Maris ends her poem powerfully as she says:

> *Living a life that matters doesn't happen by accident. It's not a matter of circumstances. It is one made of choice; one of my own choosing. I choose to live a life that matters.*

Happiness means knowing what you believe to be true about life, and it means knowing what you want for your life—and loving it! My hope is that you may be inspired to live your life consciously, fully aware of your magnificent personal power to create your life exactly as you want it to be.

ACTION STEPS:

Here is a starting point for mastering the art of living consciously.

1. Make sure that you start with the belief that you can and will learn to consciously create a life you will truly enjoy—one filled with learning, a sense of purpose, happiness, and great fulfillment.

2. Get very clear about exactly what you want in key life areas such as health, career, finances, relationships, and families. Spend a little time each day sitting in a comfortable place and thinking in detail about what you want in each key area of your life. The clearer you are and the more details you have in your head about what you want in each area, the more likely your words and actions are to follow those thoughts. You will then be more highly motivated and filled with energy as you enter into your day's activities.

3. Be aware of how your life feels to you at any given moment. Is it joyous? Are you enthusiastic as you begin each day? Are you energized by what you are doing with your life? If not, make adjustments. Your goal is happiness, and you are in the process of creating the life that will make you happy.

4. Examine old beliefs to make sure they make sense in light of your conscious intention for your life. For instance, you may have been taught to judge your personal worth by the income you make, or by your physical appearance. Consider that a life well lived has far different criteria for success. I personally consider every moment I spend feeling happy a major success.

5. Commit to high standards and personal growth as a way of life. Life is intended to feel good. Be aware of how your life feels to you at any given moment. Is it joyous? Are you energized by what you are doing with your life? If not, you will want to consider implementing some of the many suggestions in this book. Your goal is happiness, and you are in the process of creating the life that will make you happy.

Why wait? Be happy now!

We created a vision for how we wanted the rest of our life together to be and how we wanted life to feel for us despite our challenges. If he was going to experience this illness, we wanted to do it on our terms.

CHAPTER 7

I Know What I Want~And I'm Lovin' It!
(CREATING A VISION FOR YOUR LIFE)

The next step to creating a life of happiness is knowing what you want—in other words, having a vision for your life.

Right now, if someone were to ask you, "What is your vision for your life?" how would you respond? You might find yourself spending a lot of time clearing your throat, feeling embarrassed, and trying to pull a response from a mind that has gone completely blank. Very few of us have given much thought to this important question. Nor have we realized the richness, fullness, and happiness that can be experienced on a daily basis when we have a vision we feel passionately about making into reality.

Who are you and what do you want? Many of us believe that happiness lies in our accomplishments, or that the "toys" we buy ourselves will be our source of happiness, or even that happiness is found in the approval of others.

However, as author and lecturer Wayne Dyer has noted, "When you have a vision for your life that is a grand one, you will experience a joy far greater than those things that only satisfy your ego." Your vision for life as you want it to be is what gives power to the all of the thoughts, words and actions that shape your life. There is a fundamental difference between a life that just happens to you, and a life that you initiate as a result of having a vision. In the first scenario, you just react to whatever life throws your way. It's that "just keeping your head above water" thing. The key word is "react." You try to make the best of the circumstances in which you find yourself, rather than consciously creating your life as you want it to be.

If Charles and I had just reacted to life when he first got sick, we would have experienced a lot of fear, anger, and feelings of helplessness. In fact, we would probably have become stuck in that negativity and lived there for four years. I'm not saying we didn't go through a period of shock when we realized just how bad our situation was. Of course we did. But we recovered. We "got it together." We started taking charge of our lives. We created a vision for how we wanted the rest of our life together to be and how we wanted life to feel for us despite our challenges. If he was going to experience this illness, we wanted to do it on our terms. So here's how we created a vision for our life, and turned our vision into a very enjoyable life despite Charles' illness. The process looked something like this:

1. **We saw the possibility** that comes from knowing you can create a life that will bring you great joy. It was a little hard to imagine that life, in this situation, could bring us joy, but we knew that rather than spending our time down in the dumps, we wanted our days together to be filled with good times, laughter, and enjoyment of the present moment. We saw the possibility!

2. **We began to identify what pleased us most.** We started noticing all kinds of things that we valued that we wanted to include in our vision for our life together in this situation—things like laughter, friendship, locating old friends to chat with on the phone, strengthening our bonds with family and current friends, watching reruns of old sit-coms and remembering the laughter we would share as we watched those shows with our kids. Carol Burnett, Tim Conway, Dick Van Dyke, The Andy Griffith Show, All In the Family—we could put ourselves into instant good moods with any of those!

3. **We created the vision** based on the possibilities we saw, and those things we identified that we wanted our lives to be all about at this point in time.

4. **Our vision created desire**—to only live from that vision, and not sink into the hopelessness and despair that were always waiting just outside our door. Our vision for life as we wanted it to be became so compelling that we kept finding more things we wanted to include, and as we became more and more clear about what we wanted, we loved it! We were so grateful for the time we were given to enjoy living out that vision and doing the things—those "little things that mean a lot"—that created so much happiness in our lives.

5. **We "plugged in our destination"**—just like you do with your GPS—and began turning our vision into a reality. We simply started doing the things that would make our vision of a happy life a reality. By having a clear vision of what we wanted our life to look like, we created what was to become the rest of our life together—and it was a beautiful creation. Plug in your destination.

In his book, *The 7 Habits of Highly Effective People,* Stephen Covey teaches us to "begin with the end in mind," This is what having a vision is all about. Your vision is your "end in mind" that provides the roadmap for the choices you make and the actions you take on a day to day basis. It is the destination that you plug into your Emotional Guidance System (EGS). Once you have your destination (your vision) plugged in, your EGS will let you know via your emotions if you think a thought, speak a word, or take an action that is taking you off the course you have charted to reach your goal.

For example, a part of my vision for our home during those four years was "an atmosphere of kindness and compassion." When my words were harsh and cranky, I would immediately feel out of alignment, out of sorts, and pretty much just angry with myself. But by noticing my feelings, I could recognize when it was time to make some adjustments in my attitudes and/or behavior (since I am the only one whose behavior I can control), and I set about making the necessary corrections to get myself back on course.

Your vision and the destination that you plug in to your EGS doesn't have to be about your entire life (your life dream). It can be what I call a "small scale vision." It can be about the feelings you want in your home, about staying in shape, enjoying your family, or working as a "pet partner" team with your dog as you brighten the day for someone in a nursing home——whatever you want. Your vision simply needs to be a vivid description of a desired outcome that inspires you, energizes you, and helps you create a clear mental picture of what you want.

Try to capture the essence of your vision using a simple, memorable phrase. For example, I have a "small scale vision" that the relationships in my life will be warm and fulfilling." Whether I am talking to a stranger or a family member, my "end in mind" or destination is that people in my life will feel listened to and cared about. That is the outcome I want. As each interaction with another person is occurring, my emotions give me continuous feedback as to whether the person is feeling warm and good about the conversation, or feeling that I am giving less than my best to our discussion.

When I am not paying attention to the outcome I want in my conversation, I tend to multitask, or find my mind wandering, especially if I am on the telephone. When this occurs during a phone conversation with one of my daughters, I get busted every time (as I should!) because there is a different feeling to the conversation, and she definitely doesn't feel listened to. In other words, when my words and my actions don't align with my vision, I don't get the outcome I want.

A SENSE OF PURPOSE

Researchers have long noted that people often make the mistake of believing that external things are what define success and bring them the happiness they are seeking. Yet, what often happens when people have the income they want, the expensive house, or the hot sports car, is that they initially experience a sense of euphoria and excitement, but these feelings are often quickly replaced by a sense of letdown when the excitement wears off. There is a sense that there is something more to life, but rarely does anyone figure out what is missing. It is my belief that what is missing for so many people is the joy that is experienced when you have a clear vision and a strong sense of purpose for your life.

Researchers have also found that, among those people incarcerated in prison camps during World War II, having a vision and a strong sense of purpose (i.e. the desire to teach others the lessons you have learned, or the desire to be reunited with a loving family after having been separated) have been linked to amazing survival stories. The life of Dr. Viktor Frankl, a Viennese psychiatrist, and author of the book, *Man's Search for Meaning,* provides a powerful example of the importance of having a vision and a sense of meaning and purpose.

Dr. Frankl, tortured in the Nazi prison camps, never knew from one day to the next whether he would be one of those who would be sent to the gas ovens or succumb to the latest plague sweeping through the prison camp. As he endured the horrors of his circumstances, he realized that he had the freedom—perhaps man's greatest freedom—to decide how his experience was going to affect him. He had the power to choose how he would respond to these circumstances.

How he ultimately did respond was inspired by his vision for his life. Dr. Frankl pictured himself released from prison and in a classroom teaching students the profound lessons he learned while in prison. Because of his vision and commitment to the future, he remained hopeful and persevered despite the horror of his situation. He survived when others around him were dying physically, emotionally, and spiritually. Interestingly, as indicated by his ability to survive the many diseases that were experienced by other prisoners, his immune system benefitted from his vision and sense of purpose as well—a true mind/body connection. When he was finally released, he did, in fact, fulfill his vision by teaching college students about resilience based on his first-hand experiences and the profound lessons he had learned during the horror of his incarceration.

CHANGING OLD HABITS

Sometimes you might find that the vision you are shaping for yourself is going to require that you make substantial changes in your current habits—and changing old habits can be very difficult. One of the greatest lessons that I have learned from my own life experience, and the lives of people with whom I work, is that when you want to make a positive change in your life, it is extremely important that there is something you want more than your old way of doing things. That something becomes your vision, both for yourself and for your life as you want it to be.

For example, after several failed attempts in the past, I made the decision to put alcohol out of my life in 1993. This time was different. There was something I wanted more than I wanted a cocktail (or two, or three). That "something" was the me that I knew I could be without alcohol—the vision I held for my life as I knew it could be without alcohol.

My husband and I had a social life that included many cocktail parties, and even when we weren't going out, we usually had drinks before dinner. I knew that making such a drastic change in my lifestyle would be a major challenge. But, I had something going for me this time that I didn't have previously. I had a clear picture in my mind of the confident, strong, empowered, and joyous woman who knew she could do anything she could put her mind to. It was that vision—that picture of myself—that allowed me to accomplish my goal of having no alcohol in my life with great ease. I never ever wavered from my resolve. I knew the person I could become, and I wanted that person and what that person could contribute to this world far more than I wanted that next drink.

So I had the magic formula—I knew what I wanted, and I had fire in my belly—a passion and enthusiasm that came from deep within me, and propelled me forward toward the achievement of my goal. This kind of passion is the "lovin' it" part. It is the to do. When you are inspired by a vision of what is possible in your life, nothing can stand in your way. It energizes you, it affirms you, it provides you with a sense of direction, and it motivates you when the going gets tough!

KNOW WHAT YOU VALUE

In order to know what you want, it is important to know what you value. Values are the principles, beliefs, and attitudes that guide you as you make choices and decisions in life. Your core values are at the heart of who you are. When you are not in alignment with your values—when you act in a way that conflicts with your values and beliefs—your life doesn't flow easily. Happiness will seem elusive, and life will feel like one big struggle.

It is important that your vision for your life reflect your core values, the very deepest values you hold. Your core values are at the heart of who you are. They define your essence, those characteristics and values that lie deep within your heart, and form the center of your life. In the Action Steps section of this chapter you will have the opportunity to identify those core values which are most important to you. When you have identified your core values, those words (values) that ring true for you, you can then incorporate them into your vision for your life.

Once you have identified your values and life as you want it to be (your vision), the next step is to think about what you are going to do to make that vision a reality. This becomes your mission statement. Your **vision statement** is the outcome you want. Your **mission statement** is the action you need to take to fulfill that vision. For example, if your vision is that the world become a peaceful, loving and joyous place, your mission might be to educate, inspire and role model peace, love and joy for others in order to promote a peaceful, loving and joyous world. You will have an opportunity to give more thought to your vision and your mission statement in the Action Steps section of this chapter.

After you have clarified your vision and your mission (your role in fulfilling that vision), you put them into action in your life. You start noticing whether your words and actions are consistent with your values as reflected in your vision and your mission statement. All you have to do is pay attention to your emotions—your EGS. If you are at "contentment" or higher on the emotional scale, you are probably living your values. In other words, your actions and your values are in good alignment.

As I mentioned in the previous chapter, I have a daily practice for reviewing, strengthening, and expanding my own vision. I sit quietly for 20 minutes each morning and visualize in detail what I want for each aspect of my life (relationships, finances, career, health, community service, fun). Then, as I go forth into my day's activities, I am extremely clear about what I want—I am "plugged in"—and my Emotional Guidance System is ready to kick in and let me know if I am "on course" or "off course." When I go "off course," and my thoughts, words, and/or actions are deviating from the vision I have set forth for myself, my emotions set off major alarm bells. I usually experience this as feelings of anxiety, or a sense of discomfort, or even just not feeling very good about myself. When this occurs, I immediately do a quick self-scan to identify my problematic attitudes and behaviors, and as quickly as possible, make necessary adjustments.

DARE TO DREAM

Since your vision statement is designed to inspire you and motivate you, you want to base your vision statement on the best outcome possible—or even not so possible. The purpose of a vision statement is not to reflect a "pretty good" outcome, but rather to stretch your imagination and open your eyes to the possibility of an amazing outcome. Albert Einstein said, "Imagination is more powerful than knowledge. Knowledge allows you to see things as they are. Imagination allows you to see things as they could be." Don't make the mistake of placing limitations on yourself when creating a vision for your life. Stretch yourself. Dare to dream. Think big! As you begin to think in terms of what is possible, you will find doors opening. You recognize new possibilities, new ways of doing things, and suddenly you have a tremendous new source of passion and energy.

And remember—the first vision you create is just the beginning. Update it and expand it as your life evolves. Keep it in front of you. A clear vision provides hope, It creates a passion for living, and It is the light on your path to happiness. Never forget, those who have a clear vision for their life are far more likely to make their dreams a reality!

ACTION STEPS:

1. **Create your vision for your life:** In order to create your vision for your life, you want to consciously choose the values by which you want to live your life. We all absorb values and beliefs from family, friends, work colleagues, even from the media, but these values aren't necessarily those that make our hearts sing. Have a look at the list of values below. Start by circling fifteen words (values) that create a gut level reaction of pleasure. Then narrow your list to ten, then to five, and finally, prioritize and list your top three values. This exercise will provide This exercise will provide an excellent starting point for creating a vision that is powerfully aligned with your most deeply held values.

LIST OF VALUES:

Abundance
Acceptance
Accountability
Accomplishment
Accuracy
Achievement
Acknowledgement
Adaptability
Adventure
Affection
Agility
Alertness
Ambition
Anticipation
Appreciation
Assertiveness
Authenticity
Awareness
Balance
Beauty
Belonging
Blissfulness
Boldness
Bravery
Brilliance
Calm
Candor
Caring
Certainty
Challenge
Change
Character
Cheerfulness
Clarity
Cleanliness
Collaboration
Comfort
Commitment
Communication
Community
Compassion
Competence
Competition
Concentration
Confidence

Connectedness
Consciousness
Consistency
Contentment
Continuity
Contribution
Control
Conviction
Cooperation
Courage
Courtesy
Creativity
Curiosity
Daring
Decisiveness
Delight
Dependability
Desire
Determination
Devotion
Dignity
Diligence
Discipline
Discovery
Discretion
Diversity
Drive
Duty
Eagerness
Education
Effectiveness
Efficiency
Elegance
Empathy
Encouragement
Endurance
Energy
Enjoyment
Enthusiasm
Equality
Excellence
Excitement
Experience
Expertise
Exploration

Expressiveness
Fairness
Faith
Fame
Family
Fidelity
Flexibility
Flow
Focus
Forgiveness
Fortitude
Freedom
Friendship
Frugality
Fun
Generosity
Giving
Goodness
Grace
Gratitude
Growth
Guidance
Happiness
Harmony
Hard work
Health
Helping others
Heroism
Holiness
Honesty
Honor
Hopefulness
Hospitality
Humility
Humor
Imagination
Independence
Influence
Ingenuity
Inner peace
Innovation
Insightfulness
Inspiration
Integrity
Intelligence

Intensity
Intimacy
Intuitiveness
Inventiveness
Investing
Joy
Justice
Kindness
Knowledge
Leadership
Learning
Liberty
Logic
Longevity
Love
Loyalty
Make a difference
Mastery
Maturity
Merit
Mindfulness
Modesty
Money
Motivation
Non-attachment
Non-violence
Opportunity
Optimism
Order
Organization
Originality
Outcome
Passion
Peace
Perceptiveness
Perseverance
Personal growth
Pleasure
Poise
Positive Attitude
Power
Practicality
Precision
Preparedness
Presence

Preservation
Privacy
Proactivity
Prosperity
Purposefulness
Quality
Rationality
Recognition
Relationships
Reliability
Religion
Resourcefulness
Respectfulness
Responsibility
Righteousness
Risk-taking
Romance
Safety
Security
Selflessness
Self-esteem
Service to others
Simplicity
Sincerity
Skill
Status
Spirituality
Stability
Strength
Success
Taking risks
Teamwork
Tenacity
Timeliness
Tolerance
Tradition
Tranquility
Trust
Truthfulness
Understanding
Variety
Wealth
Well-being
Wisdom
Work

Donna Daisy

2. **Write your vision statement.** Keeping your top three values in mind (they represent what you are deeply committed to), write a vision statement that describes what you want the future to look like. You can write a vision statement for the world, for your life, for your family or whatever you wish your focus to be. Remember, a vision statement describes how you want the future to look. If Charles and I had written our vision statement for the time we had left together, it might have been as simple as this: "Our vision is that our lives be filled with love, laughter, and the blessings of good friends and family."

3. **Create your Mission Statement for your life.** Your mission statement describes what you want to do, for whom, and the benefit as related to making your vision a reality. It should touch upon what you want to focus on, and who you want to become as a person. Such a mission statement will provide you with a rudder to guide you as you set life goals, and make action choices in both personal and professional life.

Step One: Circle the following verbs (action words) which represent actions you might take.

advance	demonstrate	further	mold	save
affect	devise	gather	motivate	serve
alleviate	direct	generate	negotiate	share
appreciate	discover	heal	nurture	speak
brighten	educate	illuminate	persuade	uphold
build	encourage	implement	practice	utilize
cause	endow	improve	produce	validate
choose	engage	inspire	promote	value
command	enhance	involve	provide	volunteer
communicate	enlighten	labor	realize	work
compete	enliven	launch	receive	worship
complete	envision	lead	resonate	write
construct	excite	master	respect	yield
create	explore	measure	restore	defend
express	mediate	safeguard	deliver	extend
model	satisfy			

70

Now, write the three verbs (action words) which most inspire you here. (Feel free to add your own).

1. _____
2. _____
3. _____

Step Two: Write the three top values you selected in Action Step 1 here. The values that you prioritized represent your core values. Core values are the essence of you—the characteristics deep within you that are at the heart of who you are, and what you center your life around. Your core values represent what you want to teach and represent in this world. (Be sure to choose words that resonate for you, not ones you think you "should" choose).

1. _____
2. _____
3. _____

Step Three: Now, consider the target population you might wish to impact in a positive way as you fulfill your mission in life. Every mission implies that someone will be helped. Get clear on who you really want to serve, be around, inspire, learn from, and impact in a positive way. Pick a group or entity or cause you would most like to help or impact in a positive way. The target population can be yourself, your family, children, underprivileged people, your business clientele, etc.

Step Four: Using the action words, the nouns, and the target group that you identified, try writing your personal mission statement using this template:

My personal mission is to _____, _____, and _____ (your 3 action words) _____, _____, and _____ (your core values or nouns go here) for (to or with) _____ (your target population goes here) for (what purpose benefit)_____.

Using the format, I wrote my personal mission statement as follows: My mission is to educate, inspire and role model (action words) happiness, compassion and purposeful living (values) for myself and those whom my life touches (for whom) in order to promote a peaceful, loving and joyous world (for what purpose).

A negative, pessismistic mindset is a very real roadblock to happiness

and to success in whatever you try to accomplish.

What you focus on grows in your mind,

in your thoughts, and in your life.

CHAPTER 8

Shift Happens!
Change Your Thinking, Change Your Life

Your mindset is probably the number one contributor to your ability to create a life filled with happiness. It is also a major factor in whether or not you are resilient and have the ability to "bounce back" when adversity strikes. Many famous quotations, such as "As a man thinketh, so shall he be" make reference to the significance of your mindset. Yet many of us go through our lives without ever questioning or challenging how we think about things, and what we tell ourselves about the circumstances of our lives. As you read this chapter, and come to understand the importance of your mindset, you will be sharpening your ability to make the shift from feelings of pessimism, disappointment, worry and unhappiness to feelings of hope, enthusiasm, and joy.

WHAT IS A MINDSET, ANYHOW?

Your mindset is the frame of reference that shapes what you tell yourself about whether you are capable of dealing with tough situations. It shapes the content of your thoughts. You either believe in your own ability to rise above adversity, or you believe you are living life at the mercy of whatever circumstances come your way. You are either optimistic, always looking for how something can be accomplished, or pessimistic, believing that the world is not a friendly place, and things aren't likely to turn out well no matter what you do. You either view the bad things that occur in your life as a challenge to be overcome, or as a catastrophe that has the potential to ruin your life. You either have a vision for life as you want it to be, or you travel life's highways with no roadmap to guide you. You are either committed to using your mind to create a joyous, fulfilling life, or you are adrift, with your good or bad fortunes riding on which way the wind might blow.

The following concepts are particularly helpful in understanding the importance of mindset:

- It's not what happens to you in life that is important; it is what you tell yourself about what happens (your thoughts) and, as a result, how you respond.

- Your thoughts about your situation are generated by your mindset (your beliefs, your attitudes of optimism or pessimism, your feelings of control or vulnerability, your confidence in your ability to deal with life or feelings of deficiency), and will determine how you respond in any situation. They will determine whether you have the tenacity to rise above the challenges you face, or whether you are more likely to become discouraged and unhappy, ultimately giving up on your dreams and goals.

THE MAKEUP OF YOUR MINDSET

For most of us, our mindset has been constructed largely from our past experiences. For example, my current attitudes of hope, confidence, and a sense of control over my life were solidified by the four years my husband and I spent rising to the challenge of extreme adversity together.

On the other hand, a person's mindset may include negative and pessimistic thoughts and beliefs from the past such as the person trying to lose weight who has these beliefs: "I will always be fat. My mother, my grandmother and my great grandmother were all heavy, so I'll probably be just like them." These beliefs can tend to be very discouraging, and spoil any efforts at weight loss before they get of the ground.

You may also have, as a part of your mindset, a little voice in your head which is sometimes called your Critic. Your Critic is also a reflection of voices from the past—usually people who found fault with you or your behavior. Perhaps they were your parents, or your teachers, or a girlfriend or boyfriend who you wanted desperately to please. As you can imagine, your Critic heavily influences your belief in yourself by pointing out all of your shortcomings and deficiencies. It constantly reminds you of all the reasons that you cannot possibly achieve your dreams.

SOME OF THE THINGS YOUR CRITIC MIGHT SAY ARE:

> "Who are you to think you can be happy. Your mother and grandmother practically lived on anti-depressants!" or "You don't have a chance of fulfilling your vision for a life of abundance and happiness. You had better face reality, lower your expectations, and get back on safe footing."

A negative, pessimistic mindset is a very real roadblock to happiness and to success in whatever you try to accomplish. In order to overcome the negative messages from your past, it is important to identify and override the Critic's negative comments, and, instead, start nurturing the encouraging self-talk that accompanies a resilient, "bounce-back" mindset. Focus on the positive aspects of your life, and especially your own personal strengths. What you focus on grows in your mind, in your thoughts, and in your life. I love it whan my self-talk says, "You go, girl! You have what it takes to make this happen!"

ABOVE THE LINE MINDSET CHARACTERISTICS:

Just as there are above the line emotions and below the line emotions, there are also above the line mindset characteristics and below the line mindset characteristics that play a big role in the quality of your life. The above the line characteristics that pave the way for resilience and happiness include:

- A sense of self-efficacy or personal effectiveness: Your belief in your ability to rise above adversity. This is the one that says, "You go, girl. You can do this!"

- An optimistic explanatory style: What you tell yourself about things that happen to you. Optimistic self-talk lifts you up rather than pulling you down.

- The 3 C's of Hardiness: 1) a sense of **control** over your life, 2) a **commitment** to living your best life and taking responsibility for your own happiness, and 3) viewing adversity as a **challenge** that can be overcome.

- A sense of meaning and purpose: A belief that life is meaningful, and that we are all connected to something greater than ourselves.

- A clear vision of the life you want: This vision inspires you, creates enthusiasm, and drives your thoughts, words, and actions.

These same factors that are known to be strong determinants of resilience are also key factors in creating happiness on a daily basis.

On the other side of the coin, there are characteristics that researchers have found tend to weaken resilience and create roadblocks to success and happiness. Some of these characteristics are:

A low level of self-confidence (lack of belief in your ability to shape your life as you want it to be).

A pessimistic explanatory style—the belief that the world is an unfriendly place and that things are unlikely to turn out well.

- The belief that you have little control over your experience of life.

- Life lived by default with no vision to guide your actions.

- Lack of engagement with life. Being adrift in the world with no rudder to guide you.

It helps me get a better grasp on these characteristics that make up your mindset when I visualize them above the line or below the line as shown here:

"Bounce Back" Mindset of Happiness

Self-Efficacy
Realistic Optimism
3 Cs: Control, Commitment, Challenge
Vision
Meaning and Purpose

THE LINE

A Low Level of Self-Confidence
A Pessimistic Explanatory Style
Belief of Little Control Over Your Life Experiences
Life Lived by Default with No Vision to Guide One's Actions
Lack of Engagement with Life ~ Adrift with No Rudder to Guide You

AN EASY WAY TO AN ABOVE THE LINE MINDSET

Now, having said all of that, there might be an easier, less complicated way of looking at your mindset, and ultimately making the shift to a mindset that will always work in your favor if happiness is your goal. Make the shift to an above the line mindset by focusing on how you feel and the thoughts that produce those feelings. (You're getting good at this by now). Author and speaker Byron Katie sums it up quite well when she says, "People used to ask me if I was enlightened, and I would say, I don't know anything about that. I'm just someone who knows the difference between this hurts and this doesn't." When happiness is really important to you, you simply are unwilling to spend much time focusing on things that cause you to experience negative feelings.

When it comes right down to it, there really are only two basic emotions. One of them feels good, and the other feels bad. Since you want to create the feeling of happiness for yourself on a consistent basis, your job is to only think thoughts that make you feel good. While this may sound like an over simplification, I can tell you without exception, for every negative feeling you have, there is a corresponding negative thought. In like manner, for every positive feeling you have, there is a corresponding positive thought. In other words, you never have to search outside of yourself for happiness. You can bestow the gift of happiness upon yourself by consciously seeking to choose thoughts that create good feelings.

The example from my own life of choosing thoughts that create good feelings is the approach my husband and I took to our emotional well-being throughout the four years of his illness. There were so many negative things about our circumstances that we could have allowed to pull us below the line such as his inability to walk, the prospect of never being able to heal his surgical wounds, the active social life we no longer had, or the thought of living on a beautiful golf course with him only being able to watch other golfers from a wheelchair. We could have spent our time focusing on any one of those things, and lived our lives with constant feelings of frustration, anger and despair.

Or we could remind ourselves that our relationship was growing daily in trust and love, the fact that we were fortunate enough to live in a beautiful home in Florida where the weather is warm, and Charles could enjoy time in his favorite spot on the patio on a daily basis, or the fact that we have a wonderful family, and a golden retriever who provided both of us with best therapeutic services in Florida. We chose to focus on the good stuff, rather than trying to control the uncontrollable. We chose to give our attention to the only thing we had any control over—the thoughts that controlled our emotions.

The best way to stay upbeat and happy is to look for the best aspects of every single day. Look for things to appreciate. Look for things to feel good about. Charles and I realized that low moods were contagious, so we just kept reaching for better thoughts, ones that kept our spirits lifted rather than yielding to the temptation to feel sorry for ourselves.

By deliberately directing your thoughts, rather than just being a victim to whatever is going on around you, you can begin to make a substantial change in your life experience. And, by the way, the deliberate direction of thoughts is how unconditional love is achieved. When you choose to love someone unconditionally, it simply means that you pay attention only to those aspects of the other person that are loveable, and ignore those aspects that are not as loveable.

YOUR HIGHEST SELF

As you learn to consciously choose what you focus on in any situation, you are truly living from your highest self—your inner being—rather than from your ego self (that part of you that always wants to point out things that are not pleasing!). As you live more and more from your highest self, you will notice that you experience more loving feelings, more joy, and are less judgmental towards others. And the good news is that when you are living from your highest self, happiness will always be the overriding feeling that you experience.

HOLD ON TO WHAT YOU WANT

It is one thing to say, "I want to be happy," but quite another to really commit to happiness regardless of what difficulties might come your way. Holding on to what you want means that you are unwilling to be deterred from your vision of happiness. You are unwilling to compromise your happiness, even when others are complaining or the television and newspapers are relentlessly informing you of everything that has gone wrong in the world, or could possibly go wrong.

Of course, there will be circumstances and people in your life that have a high potential for bringing you below the line, away from happiness, but to the extent that you can accomplish this (and it is a skill worth mastering), ignore them! Simply do not place your attention on that which takes you away from your happiness.

THE SHIFT

The shift that you are looking for comes from 1) literally changing your thinking habits so that your thoughts are more aligned with that which produces happiness, and 2) giving less attention to the old, ego-dominated thoughts about what is missing in your life, what has happened that doesn't please you, or what isn't exactly the way you would like it to be.

I have been practicing this simple yet profound, mind strategy—this shift in the way I use my thinking—for several years, and it is amazing how much more time I spend above the line on the happiness scale. Choosing which thoughts you allow in your head, focusing only on thoughts which bring you happiness, is a major shift from the usual way most people approach life. Most of us think we are remiss if we don't work and rework problems in our head, or play over and over again conversations we had that were upsetting to us.

We even call our friends to help us add fuel to the fire in our mind about how badly we have been treated by someone else. Being stuck in thoughts of how badly you have been treated, or how unappreciated you are, or how you never seem to get the respect you want will only pull you further and further from the good feelings you are desiring to have.

DON'T FORGET YOUR EMOTIONAL GUIDANCE SYSTEM

If you wonder how you can possibly monitor your thoughts in a way that will keep you in that above the line, good feeling place, the dilemma is easily solved by getting back to a strategy mentioned earlier—paying more attention to your Emotional Guidance System. Your feelings are directly linked to your thoughts, so if you are experiencing discouragement, anger, sadness, or any of the below the line feelings, you can be sure your thoughts need a little adjustment. Thoughts of gratitude, kindness, or compassion will always bring you right back to the above the line feelings you are seeking.

As you deliberately choose the direction of your thoughts, and give your attention to thoughts that produce better feelings, you are well on your way to more and more experiences of happiness. On the other hand, if you are experiencing negative emotions, your EGS is warning you that you need to stop what you are doing or thinking about, and focus your thoughts on something that feels better.

I recognize that there are times when life requires us to take our thinking to places that are painful, such as certain business decisions, health problems, or relationship issues that must be dealt with. In those situations, a good strategy is to distance yourself from the emotional discomfort by seeing yourself as the objective observer, and making decisions from that frame of reference. Then, consciously return to the mindset that you have created for the purpose of bringing joy and a sense of well-being.

LIFE IS GOOD

As you become more committed to "being happy now," and you start making some changes in the way you use your thinking, you will begin to feel excited and enthusiastic about just how good life can feel. You will notice that your happiness remains despite all of life's ups and downs. In addition, you will probably find that you are experiencing all of the characteristics that researchers have attributed to resilient people such as optimism and a growing belief that you really do have the ability to take control of your life and your happiness.

Another thing you will notice is that as you become more proficient at focusing on only positive aspects of things, you will find yourself more and more in a state of positive feelings (happiness). You will go through life in an easier, more fluid way as you begin to make the shift towards more joy, contentment, and fulfillment in your life. You are likely to find that you have more energy, and are more engaged with your work and with other people. You're resilient, you're happy, and you are successful at reaching many of your goals. Your feelings of physical and mental well-being improve, including your feelings of self-confidence and self-esteem. And, as an added value, research has shown that happy people (people who live above the line emotionally) benefit not only themselves, but their partners, families, communities, and society at large. In short, as we increase our happiness level, we make the world a better place!

ACTION STEPS:

Action Step #1: As you are moving through your day, be sensitive to the way you feel. Start noticing when negative thoughts are pulling you away from happiness. The presence of negative thoughts is easy to identify, since you will be experiencing one or more of the below the line feelings such as disappointment, doubt, worry, frustration, anger, or fear, As you identify the thought that is pulling you toward bad feelings, write it down.

1. Next, consciously make the shift to a more positive thought (the new thought must be believable!) and write it down.

_____

2. Now write the feelings you experience as a result of the new thought.

_____

  Here is an example of how this process works:

1. Identify a thought that is pulling you into below the line feelings: Because

of my husband's illness, our life together is never going to be the same.

2. Consciously shift to a more positive thought: Everything is going to be fine. Note: That thought doesn't work because I don't believe it. So I try another thought: We may not have any control over his illness, but we can control the attitude that we bring to this situation, and we are going to make every day the best day possible!

3. Resulting feelings: Hope, determination, commitment (Notice that all of these are above the line feelings).

By reaching for, and focusing on a new thought that is believable, you can gradually begin moving toward the way you want to feel. Remember, your new thought doesn't have to provide the end-all solution. You are only looking for a thought that feels good.

Action Step #2: Sometimes situations over which you have no control have the potential to dramatically lower your spirits. In those cases, to the extent that you can, remove yourself from the constant reminders about the negative situation, and focus on something more pleasing.

For example, when the stock market news on any given day is really bad, we would check once or twice on what is happening, but then immediately turn off the TV, or at least find a fun, comedy show to watch, and take our focus off any bad financial news.

Our previous behavior was to keep watching, and feeling our blood pressure rise and our fear grow as commentators discussed everything that might possibly go wrong.

Now, our new thought process then went something like this: "We have done everything in our power to maintain a sound portfolio and we communicate with our advisor on a regular basis, so now is the time to let go and realize that while we have no control over the markets, and that whatever happens, we will be alright."

Why wait? Be happy now!

When you notice yourself experiencing any of the 'below the line' emotions such as sadness, guilt, anger or fear, notice what you are thinking, and quickly shift your thought to one that strengthens you, energizes you and restores happiness and contentment.

CHAPTER 9

Cultivate Life Skills for Happiness

When you decide you want to increase the level of happiness and well- being in your life, it sometimes feels a little overwhelming as you contemplate things you want to change. I usually find that I need some very specific new skills, and some clear ideas for how to use those skills in my life. This chapter focuses on key life areas or circumstances, and provides skills and strategies that I have found useful in my own life and the lives of others with whom I work.

I. SKILLS FOR STRENGTHENING YOUR INTENTION TO BE HAPPY

In his book, *The Power of Intention,* Wayne Dyer defines intention as a strong purpose or aim, accompanied by a determination to produce a desired result. In the words of Carlos Castaneda, "intent is a force that exists in the universe. When sorcerers (those who live of the Source) beckon intent, it comes to them and sets up the path for attainment, which means that sorcerers always accomplish what they set out to do." Once you have set your intention to be happy, you can strengthen that intention in the following ways:

1. **Monitor your thoughts.** Your intention to be happy is strengthened or weakened by your thoughts, and by what you are telling yourself about what is going on in your life. When what you are telling yourself is positive and upbeat, the feelings you will experience will be those above the line feelings described in Chapter Four. When your thoughts and your self-talk are negative (thinking about what is missing in your life, thoughts about aspects of your life that you dislike, thoughts about what others say you should be, do or feel that don't match up with your desires), you are likely to experience below the line feelings, such as self-doubt, guilt, and anxiety. In other words, once you have decided what you desire (i.e. happiness), any thought you think or action you take that is not in harmony with that intention will feel uncomfortable for you.

2. **Pay attention to your energy level.** Happiness carries with it a certain level of energy. You want to be aware of that energy level and do things that bring you to the energy level of happiness. For example, notice the energy level of the thoughts and words you use. A friend of mine, who is an excellent physician and healer, has a check list of questions she uses to review the health status of her patients. One of the questions she would ask when evaluating the person's emotional state was, "Do you have any unresolved sorrows that need to be addressed?" She began to realize that the word, "sorrows" summoned forth energy-draining thoughts of life's heavy burdens, so she changed the wording of her question to, "Does your life have the joy and fulfillment you are seeking?" The energy from that question tended to evoke a significantly different "can do" response, including, "I must quit dwelling on those things I can't fix, and get on with the business of creating a happy life."

If your thoughts are negative (complaining, justifying, blaming, feeling guilty, feeling angry), they weaken you by pulling down your energy level. Your emotions will quickly tip you off that these thoughts are not enhancing your intent for happiness. When you notice yourself experiencing any of the below the line emotions such as sadness, guilt, anger or fear, notice what you are thinking, and quickly shift your thought to one that strengthens you, energizes you, and restores happiness and contentment.

For example:
Thoughts that weaken you and lower happiness: I am so angry with my family. They don't understand me, and certainly don't treat me the way I think they should. Thoughts that strengthen you and promote happiness: My family sees things differently than I do, but I love them and understand that we are all different. I can remain focused on my intentions for happiness, while at the same time continuing to love them.

3. **Cultivate thoughts of forgiveness:** Research on muscle testing has shown that thoughts of forgiveness strengthen us, while thoughts of revenge, anger, and hatred weaken us. Simple thoughts of forgiveness, even without taking any action, raise your energy level and assists in fulfilling your intentions— in this case, happiness.

4. **Frequently focus your thoughts on kindness:** Kindness is an energizer and strengthens your intention for happiness. Unkind thoughts weaken it. As an added benefit, when you put kindness out into the universe, it tends to flow back into your life.

5. **Break the "chain of pain" from negativity:** It is easy to lose your happiness temporarily when in the company of certain people who drain your energy with their complaints about their lives. When others are telling you of their misfortunes, do not become a part of the "chain of pain" by participating in discussions focused on pain and being a sounding board for their complaints. Instead, through your words and actions, hold an image of improvement for them, and help them move toward that higher place. I like to think of this analogy when applying this strategy: Imagine that you were walking on a mountain and fell over the ledge. The only thing keeping you from falling was a very flimsy vine which you grabbed. Who would you prefer to be there for you—a friend who was weak and not focused or one who was strong and sure footed? Be that strong person for your friend with difficulties. Focus on positive aspects and well-being, and call your friend to that better-feeling place.

II. SKILLS FOR INCREASING HAPPINESS IN YOUR RELATIONSHIPS

Healthy relationships, whether romantic or friendly, tend to be critical factors in our level of happiness. They also appear to be bidirectional. That is, when you have healthy romantic relationships and friendships, you tend to be happier, and happy people more easily acquire lovers and friends. Sounds like the chicken and egg thing! Nonetheless, since there is such a high correlation between happiness and relationships, it is a good idea to make the cultivation of skills that promote healthy relationships (both with your friends and with your spouse or lover) a high priority. Here are some strategies you might find helpful.

1. **Pay attention to the way you communicate:** All relationships, whether business relationships or intimate ones, grow stronger and happier when you care about and pay attention to the way you communicate. When you communicate effectively, you are better able to handle adversity, deal with stress, and resolve difficult situations. Communication has many components, including a verbal component (what you say and how you say it), a listening component (listening, hearing, and understanding), and a non-verbal component (your body language, eye contact, and actions). Have you ever had someone say to you, "I can tell just by looking at you that you're upset?" I certainly have! Actions really do speak louder than words! If you want to increase your sense of personal control and effectiveness, try examining the way you communicate. Examples of effective communication include being able to express your likes and dislikes, knowing how to accept a compliment, and knowing when to say "yes" and when to say "no"—and mean it! The way people respond to you is almost always directly correlated with how you communicate. The communication of people who are truly effective is usually open, honest, and appropriate, typically enhancing self-esteem and nurturing relationships. The communication of less effective people often tends to be in a style of blaming, denying, and attacking. Needless to say, that style of communication is damaging to your self-esteem and to your relationships. It also tends to contribute to a high level of stress in your life.

2. **Be aware of your communication styles:** Many of us have grown up in family situations where we didn't learn the importance of good communication skills, and certainly didn't see them modeled. Yet, the style we use to communicate with others often determines how effective we are in both our business and personal relationships. In the examples of communication styles shown below, you will probably recognize some people you know. Aggressive communication: This form of communication gives the message, "I am important, but you aren't," and is usually characterized by running roughshod over others, with little concern for their rights or well-being. People who use an aggressive communication style express their feelings and opinions, and advocate for their needs in a way that violates the rights of others.

Aggressive communicators are frequently verbally or physically abusive. Their standard operating procedure is best described as, "I'm superior and I'll get my way no matter what." Passive-aggressive communication: The message in this communication style is, "I am important and you aren't important, but I'm not going to tell you that." Passive-aggressive communicators are likely to smile and agree with you, but sabotage you behind your back. While appearing passive on the surface, they are really acting out anger in a subtle, indirect, or behind-the-scenes way. They typically feel powerless, resentful, and incapable of dealing directly with the object of their resentments. People who use this style of communication often have difficulty acknowledging their anger, use sarcasm, deny that there is a problem, and use subtle sabotage to get even.

Passive Communication: This is the communication of the victim who never advocates for himself. It gives the message, "you're the one who is important. I am not important." Passive communication is a style in which individuals have developed a pattern of avoiding expressing their opinions and feelings, or asking for what they need. A passive communicator operates from the belief, "I'm unable to stand up for my rights."

There is another, more effective communication style called **Assertive Communication.** Assertive Communication: Assertiveness is the ability to express your needs and rights, and your positive or negative feelings without violating the rights or limits of others. It gives the message that all are important. People who use this communication style clearly state their opinions, and they also express their needs and feelings appropriately and respectfully. They are good listeners and maintain good eye contact. They speak in a calm, clear tone of voice, and connect well with others. They stand up for their rights and do not allow others to abuse them. The motto of the assertive communicator would be, "I can't control others, but I can control myself. I am 100% responsible for my own happiness and for getting my needs met in a respectful manner." They place a high priority on having their rights respected and believe that all parties are equally entitled to express themselves respectfully to one another. Aggressive communication, passive-aggressive communication, and passive-aggressive communication are all communication styles typically used by people experiencing low self-esteem and lacking in the skills necessary to express their views, wants and needs in an effective manner. Assertive communication, on the other hand, is an emotionally honest, healthy communication style typically found in emotionally healthy, confident, effective people. It is easy to become so emotionally hooked in a situation that you don't share your feelings openly, or you don't really hear what the other person is trying to communicate to you. Training in self-assertion contributes greatly to a personal sense of control by helping you become more aware of your own needs and values, and learning to express them with honesty and kindness. You can often find excellent tips for self-assertion by using a search engine and putting in key words such as "how to be more assertive."

HERE ARE SOME TIPS THAT I HAVE FOUND HELPFUL FOR INCREASING ASSERTIVENESS SKILLS:

1. When you want to approach someone whose behavior you would like to see changed, stick to the facts regarding what they have done that has upset you, rather than blaming and judging the other person. Describe the behavior you want changed, how it affects you, and ask for the behavior you want. For example, your friend is consistently late when you meet for lunch:

   Inappropriate: I can't believe you're late again. You are so rude.

Appropriate assertive communication: When you arrive late for our lunches, I have to wait and I feel really frustrated. I need you to start arriving on time, or let me know if you are going to be late. Using "you" phrases ("you're so rude") comes off as judgmental and attacking, and tends to put the other person on the defensive. By using "I" statements (I feel frustrated), you are focusing on how you are feeling and how you are affected by their behavior.

2. Use a firm, but pleasant tone, looking the person in the eye.

3. Respect the other person by listening and asking questions.

4. Think in terms of how each of you can get your needs met.

5. Encourage the other person to express his or her feelings.

THE IMPORTANCE OF POSITIVE INTERACTION IN RELATIONSHIPS

According to researchers such as Sonja Lyubomirsky, author of the book, *The How of Happiness,* happy relationships are characterized by positive interactions (words and affect) by a ratio of five to one. What this means is that for every one negative interaction (criticizing, lecturing, etc.), there are five positive ones (encouragement, appreciation, affection, etc.).

Stephen Covey, author of *The Seven Habits of Highly Effective People* used the term Emotional Bank Accounts to describe how these positive and negative interactions work. He compared Emotional Bank Accounts (EBA) to financial bank accounts, explaining that you have an EBA with each person with whom you interact, and you want to always keep track of your deposits, withdrawals, and the balance in your account with that person. A positive interaction with a person would be considered a deposit; a negative interaction a withdrawal. To strengthen a relationship, it is necessary to have substantially more deposits than withdrawals.

Since the likelihood that you will marry or be involved in an intimate relationship is quite high (90% of the adult population eventually marry), it is particularly important that you hone your skills that strengthen intimate relationships. The skills for strengthening relationships suggested below are adapted from Dr. Lyubomirsky's book, *The How of Happiness,* and are equally applicable to relationships with close friends and family members.

1. **Commit extra time each week to the relationship:** If you are in a committed romantic relationship, carve out a time each day that allows you to talk—a lot! Share your plans, your hopes, and your fears. What you do or talk about isn't important. What matters is that you create a ritual of reserving time together on a regular basis.

2. **Eliminate the media:** No TV and no newspapers when you talk. Instead, listen deeply and non-judgmentally to what one another has to say.

3. **Emphasize positive communication:** Keep the five to one ratio in mind (5 positive interactions for every negative one). When you start paying attention to the quality of your interactions, you may discover that you need to increase the amount of positive affect expressed by you in your relationships. Try expressing appreciation or gratitude for specific qualities or behaviors of the other. Show appreciation. Give genuine praise when appropriate.

4. **Be happy for one another's good fortune and success.** Be happy for each other's successes. One of the distinguishing things between good relationships and those that aren't so good is not how people react to the other's bad news; it is how they react to news of success or good fortune. Responding to each other's successes with interest and enthusiasm increases intimacy and trust in the relationship. Listen. Pay attention. Ask questions.

5. **Consider "fighting differently."** Research has shown that happy couples don't necessarily fight less often or less loudly. They just fight differently. During disagreements, unhappy couples often do things that undermine healthy discussion, such as engaging in sarcasm, criticism, accusation, name calling, eye-rolling, and stonewalling (disengaging, tuning out, leaving the room). Happy couples, on the other hand, tend to do little things that de-escalate the disagreement, such as saying something like, "I see your point," finding humor or expressing affection for their partner.

BUILDING HAPPINESS INTO YOUR RELATIONSHIP WHEN YOU RETIRE:

I once heard a comedian say, "There is good news and bad news about retirement. The good news is that you get to spend more time with your spouse. The bad news is that you get to spend more time with your spouse!"

When couples retire, even if they live in the most elegant of settings, it isn't unusual for them to experience strain in their relationship. Roles have changed. The income and perks from previous jobs are gone and your parenting responsibilities are usually pretty much a thing of the past. After a while, golf every day isn't as satisfying as expected and finding interesting things to talk about at dinner each evening is becoming a struggle.

To make matters worse, most couples have never spent so much time together, and in such immediate proximity. It is easy for couples to become angry, frustrated, and irritable as they find themselves together twenty four hours a day, seven days a week, without having ever considered how their relationship and their lives should look in this new situation.

If you and your partner are looking toward retirement, you have some decisions to make. You can choose to make no preparations, maintain old patterns of interacting that aren't working for you any longer, and risk experiencing the disappointment and lack of fulfillment that comes from living out your retirement in quiet desperation. Or, you can choose to recommit to a new life and to your partner, with each of you sharing the responsibility for maximizing happiness, and making retirement the fun, exciting, joyous segment of your life that you have always envisioned.

When my husband and I retired, we had an unusual amount of challenges due to his serious health problems. He was faced with finding a way to be happy despite his illness, and I was coming to grips with being thrust into the role of full-time caregiver. Below are some of the skills and strategies that we found helpful as we dealt with retirement and the particular set of problems we faced. You don't have to wait until retirement to start using these skills. They are helpful in any committed relationship at any time of life.

1. Establish one or more shared goals such as rebuilding a healthy, mutually enjoyable relationship, and creating a happy, fulfilling retirement life for both individuals.

2. Establish that each partner is interested in the well-being of the other—not just "my way or the highway!"

3. Prioritize time for communication. No distractions—no TV—no newspaper.

4. Make communication safe so that each person is assured of not being criticized or demeaned.

5. Begin with the end in mind. When interacting, keep the focus on what you are trying to accomplish (a healthy, mutually enjoyable relationship and a fulfilling retirement). Choose words carefully rather than reacting with anger and sharp, critical words.

6. Establish ground rules for communication. The rules can be as simple as:

   - Treat each other with respect.

   - No hurtful criticisms.

   - No passive-aggressive behavior.

   - Listen deeply and without judgment to what the other is saying.

   - Think before you speak.

7. Discuss issues that are important to the relationship such as:

   - How is our marriage doing?

   - How is our retirement going?

   - How much time do we want to spend together and separately? It is important that each person maintain their sense of individuality. You need a combination of time spent together, and time spent doing things with others.

   - Who is responsible for what? Who does the grocery shopping? Who does the cleaning? Who plans the social calendar?

   - What are the financial issues that need to be discussed?

8. Build and maintain intimacy. Couples build strong relationships by creating and maintaining intimacy, and this starts with the ability to talk deeply to one another. Intimacy is the ability to be emotionally honest—to talk about what is inside you. This comes from creating a safe emotional environment where each can share his or her deepest feelings—and feel safe doing it. Intimacy is real interaction between two people where you talk about your

fears, your hopes, what is good for each of you, and what is important at each stage of life.

HOW TO COMMUNICATE WITHOUT BLAME:

One of the biggest pitfalls in the creation of harmonious and intimate relationships is blame. Kathlyn Hendricks, Ph.D. and Gay Hendricks, Ph.D. specialize in creating harmony and intimacy in relationships. They believe the following tips to be the top five skills for communicating without blame.

1. **Listen generously.** Really hear what the other person has to say.

2. **Speak unarguably.** Use statements of fact that your partner can't argue with. Example: "I feel bad when you leave for work without saying goodbye."

3. **Focus on appreciation:** Maintain a 5 to 1 ratio of statements of appreciation to complaint. Focus on the things you like about your partner and the relationship.

4. **Turn your complaints into requests.** For example, ask your partner, "If I make dinner, will you clean up?"

5. **Shift from blame to wonder.** Shift the emphasis from needing to be right and blaming your partner, to asking questions what will help create a healthier relationship.

In short, what will bring greatest harmony to any relationship is the attention by both to the desire for a healthy, mutually enjoyable relationship, and the communicating in a manner that is focused on a mutual goal, feels safe to both people, conveys appreciation of one another, and is respectful of all points of view.

III. SKILLS FOR NURTURING SOCIAL RELATIONSHIPS (FRIENDSHIPS)

Social support has long been recognized as one of the greatest buffers against stress. I think of social support as the presence of others in your life who care about you, who you can count on for help, and who will truly listen to you (and you, in turn, listen to them). Because friendship is such a key factor in feelings of happiness and fulfillment, it is important to nurture such friendships in your life. Here are some ways to do that:

1. **Make time for your friends:** As in a committed relationship with a life partner, healthy friendships need to be prioritized and nurtured. To the extent you can, plan special joint activities such as having lunch together on a regular basis, or going to the gym together, or walking your dogs together. These activities can include one or more friends. My "dog friends" and I enjoy our ritual of taking our dogs to Starbucks (the outside seating) each Sunday morning (the dogs get the whipped cream, the people get the mocha!), followed by a long walk around a small lake. It is a weekly activity that we all prioritize and only miss if we are ill or out of town. This ritual charges my battery for a full week!

2. **Share information with your friends.** Although sharing your private thoughts and feelings can be difficult for some, honest self-disclosure done in an appropriate manner cultivates trust and intimacy that can last a lifetime. I found that sharing my hopes and fears with my friends throughout the four years of my husband's illness provided a major source of therapy and healing for me.

3. **Demonstrate loyalty.** Healthy friendships thrive on loyalty and thoughtfulness. Support your friends when they need it. Honor the confidentiality of things you are told, and stand up for them when they aren't present to defend themselves, even if it isn't an action that brings you the greatest popularity at the moment.

4. **Don't forget to hug.** In my experience, hugs are one of the greatest prescriptions for wellbeing. They have a very therapeutic effect for most people, in addition to promoting intimacy, friendship and happiness. My favorite "hug experience" is the morning hug I share with my 96 year old friend, Sylvia, each day when we are both out for our walks. Those hugs have an amazingly energizing effect on both of us, and get the day off to a wonderful start.

IV. Skills for Maintaining Happiness While Coping With Stress and Adversity

Each of us have our own way of coping with the hurt or stress we experience in our lives, while at the same time trying to maintain the happiness we desire. Dr. Sonja Lyubomirsky describes two major coping styles to help us effectively handle difficult or painful situations: Problem-focused coping and Emotion-focused coping.

- **Problem-focused coping:** This type of coping involves addressing the situation by taking it into your own hands, coming up with a strategy, making a plan, and resolving it by acting on it or making it go away. For example, a couple who is preparing for retirement might anticipate the strain that is frequently placed on the relationship during retirement, and read articles and seek advice for proactively anticipating potential problems, and discussing ways of addressing these issues before they become problematic.

- **Emotion-focused coping:** In certain cases, such as the death of my husband, the only things that could be controlled in that situation were my emotions, thus the need for emotion-focused coping. This type of coping is appropriate when, as in my situation, you have no control over the circumstances, or when you are experiencing such strong negative emotions that you are temporarily unable to take action. You might opt for behavioral strategies such as distraction that helps lift your spirits such as exercise or the distraction of a good movie, or seeking the support of friends or family.

- Another choice would be **cognitive strategies** such as trying to **reframe the situation by changing your perspective.** Here's a simple example of this type of strategy: You find yourself in a traffic jam that has you at a standstill. If it is 7:45 A.M., and you are on your way to an 8 o'clock meeting, you might react by thinking, "Oh no! I'm going to be late! This is the story of my life. Whatever can go wrong, does. My boss will be furious. I may even get fired." Your body is tense, your blood pressure rises, and you notice the beginnings of a throbbing headache. An alternative approach, since you have no control over the situation, would be to say to yourself, "Since there is nothing I can do about this situation, I might as well call the office, and then relax and enjoy the new CD I just bought." In both cases, you are dealing with the same event. By making the choice to relax, however, you have empowered yourself by changing your frame of reference, and avoiding a huge amount of stress and the accompanying negative effects.

- Another helpful **cognitive strategy** is looking for the **benefit in the difficult situation.** If my husband and I had been told that we were going to have to spend four years together, day and night, coping with one horrendous challenge after another, we would have both probably said, "Just shoot me!" Yet, as the four years unfolded, the surprising benefit was that our love for one another and the feelings of trust and appreciation in our relationship grew beyond anything we had ever experienced previously. We spoke many times about what a complete surprise, and definite benefit, these emotional experiences in the midst of such difficulties were for both of us.

V. Skills for Renewing Your Energy

In a fast-paced world of demanding jobs, challenging relationships, and endless "to do" lists, we expend huge amounts of energy. If we don't take time to renew our energy, we will quickly burn out, and the toll on our happiness level will be great. As you are in the process of creating your life as you want it to be, it is essential to take charge of your life, and make time for energy renewal.

Four ways to set the stage for energy renewal are:

- learning to say no,
- setting boundaries,
- getting rid of energy drains, and
- adding energy fuels

Here is an energy analogy that works well for me. Just as a car needs fuel (gas) to run, picture yourself as needing fuel (energy) to do your daily activities. Now, imagine that each time someone asks you to do something, you reduce your fuel supply. As people ask you to do more and more, you keep reducing your fuel supply, until there is nothing left. You are running on empty. Can you imagine what happens if you are constantly giving out energy, but never replenishing it? Suddenly, your tank is empty. You are exhausted, stressed out, and burnt out. There is nothing more to give. Your fuel (energy) tank must be refilled on a regular basis. You refill your tank by learning to nurture yourself and becoming a good steward of your life energy.

You make conscious choices about how your energy will be used, and you make sure your tank gets refilled.

LEARN TO SAY NO

One way to keep your tank from getting depleted is to learn to say "no" to things that aren't important to you. Regardless of how busy or overwhelmed we are, many of us have a hard time saying "no" when we are asked by our friends, family members, and colleagues at work to take on "just one more thing." Women, in particular, get caught up in wanting to please, and in feeling guilty if they say "no."

Think about all the times that you would have liked to say "no" in a situation, but feared that you would be thought of as selfish if you did. I have struggled with that one most of my adult life. Over the years, as I worked with people who needed to learn the art of saying "no" to demanding friends and family members, unwelcome invitations, requests for money, annoying phone solicitations and much more. I would ask them to practice saying no to each request made of them that was not something they really wanted to do. The more they practiced, the more they began to reap the benefits of saying no such as more family time, or more time for themselves. They also increased their comfort level while saying no.

A primary cause for experiencing difficulty saying no is guilt. I have found that it is easier saying no if you have a history of caring and generosity toward others. If you are frequently helpful and available to your friends, family members, and co-workers, you will be able to say no when you need to with greater ease and confidence, and experience considerably less guilt.

We often get so caught up in thinking that we have to justify saying "no" that we don't think about the toll that trying to please everyone else takes on our energy and health.

In fact, if we don't learn to say "no", we could find ourselves well on our way to becoming a great doormat. A good principle to remember when saying "no" is that less is better. Don't feel compelled to go into detail about why you are saying "no." Many times, the more information you supply, the more likely the other person will be to, 1) "solve the problem" that you cite as getting in the way of you saying "yes", 2) decide your reason wasn't good enough, or 3) catch you in a lie (if that is the case).

Tell the Truth When Saying No

I have found that it is very important to tell the truth when I need to say "no." If you stick with the truth, you avoid embarrassing situations, and you feel good about yourself. Taking care of yourself is a valid reason for saying "no" that needs little explanation. Some simple phrases that can prove helpful when saying "no" are: "I have a previous engagement" or "I have plans." When I need to say "no," I often just say, "I have another obligation"—and that is true. I have an obligation to my health and well-being.

Another helpful strategy is to buy yourself some time. In order to take the pressure off when you are having trouble figuring out how to say no (or deciding what your answer will be), buy yourself some time before responding to requests. Say something like, "Let me get back to you on that."

One more helpful strategy is to "have a policy." For example, when someone wants to borrow money, and you would prefer not to lend it, it is helpful to respond by saying, "I'm sorry, but I have a policy about lending money." Having a policy implies that you have given previous thought to the issue of lending money, or learned from experience that lending money isn't a good idea.

Remember, energy is a key ingredient to happiness and success. You preserve your energy when you expend energy only on that which is of value to you. Decide which people and which projects will get your energy by asking yourself, "Does saying "yes" to this contribute to my sense of well-being? Does saying "yes" reflect what I value? Is this related to my high priority goals?" Then say "no" to the rest. And by the way, regardless of which approach you use to say "no," your assertive communication skills will come in handy.

SET BOUNDARIES

You can also use your assertive communication skills to set personal boundaries. Boundaries are your rules for what other people may and may not say or do to you.

The purpose of having boundaries is to protect and take care of yourself. Boundaries are a vital step in taking responsibility for yourself, and re-establishing and/or maintaining happiness and well-being in your life.

You need to be able to tell other people when they are acting in a way that isn't acceptable to you. Setting appropriate boundaries for other people's behavior is a "must" for maintaining a sense of control over your life. Mastering the art of setting boundaries is a necessary step in learning to take care of yourself, and letting others know that you deserve and demand respect. A boundary is like an emotional immune system. Your physical immune system protects you from invaders such as bacteria, viruses, and parasites. Your emotional immune system protects you from invasions from the words and behaviors of others.

For example, you may have some people in your life who are physically or verbally harmful. You may have others who constantly blame you, put you down, or reprimand you. Someone else may make fun of you in front of others, or discount you or challenge everything you do. It is essential that you assertively let these people know that it's not okay to treat you that way.

When setting boundaries with someone who yells at you and demeans you, you need to be able to communicate how person's behavior is affecting you, and do so without blaming ("You make me so angry.") You might say, "It's not OK to talk to me that way," followed by this formula:

> "When you _____ (describe the unacceptable behavior) I feel _____ (describe how the other person's behavior makes you feel). I need you to _____ (describe the desired behavior)."

> So you might say, When you yell at me and criticize me, I feel devalued and unloved. "I need you to discuss your concerns with me in a calm, clear way that allows us to work constructively toward a solution for this problem."

Some boundaries are non-negotiable: "It is not OK to hit me." The final part of setting boundaries is to describe what you will do to defend the boundary (i.e. the consequences).

> "If you _____ (describe the unacceptable behavior), I will _____ (describe the action you will take to protect yourself if the person violates your boundary)."

> You might say, "If you ever hit me again I will call the police and press charges. If you continue to threaten me I will call the police and press charges, and I will also get a restraining order, and defend myself in whatever manner necessary."

Always know what actions you are prepared to take in the event the other person doesn't respect your boundaries. In other words, you are willing to do whatever it takes to enforce the boundaries you set.

In a situation where your safety isn't threatened, but you are requesting a behavior change, it is a good idea to set boundaries that allow for gradual change. When setting boundaries, and describing consequences, make sure that you can live with and are prepared to uphold those consequences. Remember, setting boundaries is not a threat.

It is clear communication of consequences in the event the other person continues the unacceptable behavior.

For example, if a person is stonewalling, and avoiding the discussion of a problem by getting angry and leaving the room, you might say,

"When we are discussing our finances and you leave the room, **I feel** upset and frustrated that you are unwilling to talk with me. **I need you** to communicate with me, and help me understand if I have done something to upset you." **If you leave the room again when we are talking,** I will confront you about your behavior, and tell you how I feel.

If you continue the behavior, I will confront your behavior, and insist that we seek help for our relationship.

If you still continue that behavior, I will then assume that we are unlikely to achieve a healthy relationship, and I will consider my options, including leaving the relationship. When people refuse to respond to your boundaries and your requests, it is often wise to detach and end an unhealthy relationship.

GETTING RID OF OTHER ENERGY DRAINS

All of us have many things that drain our energy. Sometimes we aren't even consciously aware of our energy drains. Some of the things that most noticeably drain our energy are:

- worry

- resentment

- unmet emotional needs

- unhealthy eating habits

- unpaid bills

- clutter

- lack of financial reserves

- unhealthy relationships

- lack of exercise, and

- work you don't enjoy

Think about the energy drains in your life. Once you have identified them, you can prioritize the ones you need to eliminate from your life, and start getting rid of them.

WAYS TO FUEL YOUR ENERGY

As you start eliminating energy drains from your life, you will want to also start thinking about things that fuel your energy. Your objective is to always know how full your "tank" is and to keep doing the things that you know will rejuvenate your energy. Consider replenishing your energy on a regular basis by building relaxation into your schedule, as well as maintaining a healthy diet, exercising on a regular basis, and developing a network of family and friends who you can turn to in times of need. Seek out those people who uplift you, and connect with your own spirituality.

ADDITIONAL IDEAS FOR REFUELING YOUR ENERGY:

- Take a walk.

- Get rid of clutter (clean out a closet, organize your desk, etc.).

- Spend time with people who make you laugh.

- Take time for simple pleasures.

- Share your life with a pet that loves you. It has been said that until one has loved an animal, a part of their soul remains unawakened. (Anatole France)

- Have work that is meaningful and connected to your vision for your life.

- Maintain a financial reserve.

- Cultivate your sense of humor.

As you begin getting rid of things that drain your energy and you build energy boosters into your life, you will be amazed at how energized you will feel and how well you will be able to focus on doing the things that support your priorities, including your intention for happiness.

VI. GOAL SETTING: AN IMPORTANT PART OF HAPPINESS

Jim Cathcart, a noted professional speaker, once said, "Most people aim at nothing in life, and hit it with amazing accuracy." If you don't have a clear vision of what you want in your life, it's very hard to hit the mark. Identifying and working toward a valued goal that is personally meaningful for you is one of the most important things you can do if you want to increase your happiness level. Goals represent your hopes and dreams.

They excite you. They motivate you. When you think about it, the unhappiest people around you—those who are the least enthusiastic about life, the most negative, bored, and least motivated—are usually those who have no life goals that they are trying to achieve. According to happiness expert, Dr. Sonja Lyubomirsky, some of the benefits those folks, and all of us, would gain if they choose to identify and pursue even one meaningful goal are:

- Finding the sense of purpose derived from committed goal pursuit.

- Boosts in self-esteem which are enhanced along the way by the accomplishment of sub-goals.

- Added structure and meaning to daily life.

- Learning the art of mastering the use of time.

- Engagement with other people (friends, teachers, colleagues and partners) during the achievement of the goal.

In my personal experience, I had an additional benefit to having goals. Early on in my husband's illness, I knew that I had a long-range goal of writing a book, and sharing with others our experience and how we survived and thrived emotionally. Just the idea of focusing on what Charles and I were learning, and the benefit these lessons could bring to others created tremendous warmth in my heart. However, while my time and energy were so consumed with the necessary care-giving, I found it necessary to break things down into smaller, but related goals. I was able to find time to write short articles about our experiences for eBella magazine, and just putting those articles on paper carried with it the powerful therapeutic effect of journaling. Then, when I was able to pursue the big dream—this book—my eBella articles became useful reference points for many sections of the book.

Research has shown that goals that are personally involving and rewarding, such as putting your life experiences in writing, are more likely to be significant contributors to happiness than pursuits that reflect the goals of others. For example, while growing up. I pursued many goals such as math and music contests, performances in dance recitals, and academic achievements. But these goals were based more on what my parents wanted for me than anything I had chosen based on my own values. The achievement of those goals did provide me with a tremendous sense of confidence, and did wonders for my self-esteem. Those pursuits were also how I learned to prioritize and plan the use of my time each day. While they didn't necessarily bring me the deep joy that I am experiencing from the achievement of this particular intrinsic goal (the writing of this book), they certainly prepared me in many ways (confidence, competence, organization) to pursue many more satisfying goals later in life.

The pursuit of meaningful goals is particularly important when you retire or if you are disabled, or limited by health issues. It's not only provides you an opportunity to master new skills, you also are likely to enjoy increased social interaction with people sharing similar interests. Another benefit of engaging in activities you deeply value, such as charitable fund raising, working with Habitat for Humanity, volunteering with the local Humane Society, even enrolling in online classes that are of interest to you, is that it provides you the structure and sense of purpose you may have enjoyed in your work life.

VII. Skills for Managing Your Finances

Attitude management

While it is said that money doesn't buy happiness, sound financial management is a critical skill for promoting a sense of control that contributes significantly to feelings of well-being. Lack of money, on the other hand, can bring about stress, emotional pain and unhappiness. As with anything else, your attitude about money is a key contributor to your relationship with money. Just as you have a relationship with your friends, your husband, your children, and other relatives, you also have a relationship with money. You have attitudes about it. You love it (it feels so good when you have it)—you hate it (when you don't have enough)—you may even fear it (losing it). You also have some pretty deeply engrained beliefs about money. You believe you have enough; you believe you will never have enough. Whatever you tell yourself about money is very likely to end up being what you experience about money. Most of us have "our stories" that brought us to how we feel about money. I certainly have one, and I want to briefly share that story with you. Charles always managed our money and our investments and did a good job. I didn't get involved because my philosophy was that a ship only needs one captain—a kitchen only needs one chef. When Charles became ill, we both realized that I needed to learn where our money was invested, why it was invested the way it was, and how he made certain financial decisions. Over time, I learned all of this and even developed my own working relationship with the advisors that handled out assets. After Charles died, however, I discovered that even though I had learned most everything I needed to know about the mechanics of managing our money, what I wasn't counting on was the impact of my own belief system around money—my own fears about poverty which were based on my family history. Even though I was financially comfortable at the time, I found that I had a great fear that it wouldn't be enough—especially with the economic situation and the decline in the stock market we had recently experienced. I was so fearful that I was hoarding every penny I could. I was passing up opportunities to go out with my friends because I was afraid to spend the money. I finally had one of our advisors do projections and lay everything out for me, and yet I still had this underlying immobilizing fear—what some people call a scarcity mentality. So I bought every book I could find and I did a lot of research about the impact of a person's beliefs on the ease with which money flows into their life (and goes out!).

What I learned was that the way we think and feel about money can either help us or hinder us from having what we want and enjoying what we have. In the words of Suze Orman, "Our thoughts and feelings about money are fundamental factors in determining how much money each of us will, in this lifetime be able to create and keep."

Henry Ford once said, "Whether you believe you can or you believe you can't, you're usually right." And this statement is particularly true when it comes to your money. We all have attitudes and beliefs that determine our mindset about money. To have more, you have to begin by thinking you can have more. Whether you realize it or not, you probably spend quite a lot of time talking to yourself or someone else about your relationship with money. Have you ever really noticed what words you choose? Do you tend to say, "I'll never have enough money to do the things I want to do." (I did!) or "I can't afford that!" (I did!) If these are the kinds of words you use in connection to money, you may have what we call a scarcity mentality. If, on the other hand, you use words like "I'm learning to manage my money quite well," or "I always seem to have enough money to do the things I want," you are probably pretty comfortable in your relationship with money, and believe in your ability to create wealth. If these things are true about you, you have an abundance mindset. I was introduced to the term "abundance mentality" by author Dr. Stephen Covey when I read his book, *The Seven Habits of Highly Effective People.* Covey states that an abundance mentality is the belief that there is enough out there for everyone. He suggests that when we grasp that concept, we no longer will feel compelled to compete for our resources and hoard them.

Instead, we begin to think in terms of sharing—money, prestige, recognition—everything. With that shift in our thinking, we begin to see new possibilities, new alternatives, and new opportunities in our everyday lives. I am only just now coming to understand the difference in an approach to money and to life that comes from a scarcity mentality, and an approach that comes from an abundance mentality. In my mind, the picture I hold of someone with a scarcity mentality is that of someone grasping, clinging, and thinking only of themselves. The picture I have of an abundance mindset is more that of someone in a bountiful garden, filling their basket with never ending fruits, vegetables and flowers—anything they want. In Covey's terms, people with an abundance mindset are those who regularly engage in a "win-win" approach to every aspect of their lives, both personal and professional. Many of us are scripted from childhood into a scarcity mentality, particularly if we happened to be around during the Great Depression. The financial crisis in recent years has also played a role in keeping our thoughts of fear and scarcity activated. I would like to encourage you to join me in cultivating an abundance mentality. Start to believe that we can all learn to work together, knowing that there is plenty for everyone if only we will start to approach our challenges, big and small, with a win-win attitude. With such an attitude, we will soon start discovering ways to educate and feed more people on our planet. We will learn to help others meet their needs and fulfill their goals, even as we are expanding our own lives. People with a scarcity mentality play small in life. They are frequently suffering from low self-esteem and often set low goals for themselves. If they do set high goals, they rarely succeed. On the other hand, people with an abundance mentality, and a win-win approach to life, find it easy to rise to life's challenges. They play a larger game. In doing so, they tend to attract the people and opportunities into their lives that will assist them in the achievement of their goals, and in making their vision for life a reality.

MONEY MANAGEMENT:

Many of us have never had even basic training in the art of managing money. Without the skills necessary for effective money management, you can find yourself buried in debt, and dealing with emotional issues such as anxiety about where your money goes, worry about if there is enough money, and feelings of hopelessness about your ability to improve your financial situation. As with everything else we have covered, the key to financial success lies in you taking responsibility—in this case, taking responsibility for your financial well-being.   Regardless of how much money you make, or how much money it takes for you to live, the following fundamental financial principles will help you achieve financial success:

Know how much money you need to do what you want to do and have what you want to have. By doing this, you are better able to make choices consistent with your values and needs. In our consumer culture, we tend to believe that more is better, so we work extended hours, trying to make more. Instead, start by calculating how much is enough—for you! You may be astounded to see how little you need in order to do what you want and have what you want.

Live within your means. Compare the money you have coming in with the money you have going out (real income, real expenses). Spend less than you make. When you live within your means you buy only what you can afford. When you spend beyond your means, you pay a huge interest penalty for the purchases you make and the debt burden grows deeper and deeper.

Know your credit score. Your credit score is a numerical computation that provides potential lenders information regarding how risky it might be to lend you money.   The most commonly used credit score is known as your FICO Score. (FICO is short for Fair Isaac and Co.). The Fair Isaac Company developed custom software back in the 1980s that helped other companies determine a credit risk based on a number derived from a person's credit history, including payment history, amounts owed, length of credit history, new credit, and types of credit used. This number soon became a standard that was adopted by the three main credit bureaus: Experian, TransUnion, and Equifax. The FICO score ranges between 300 and 850. A good credit score (what potential lenders are looking for) is considered to be 700 or above.

Build a reserve. Save for a rainy day. When you build a financial reserve, you have a bucket of money to draw from when times are tough, when unexpected expenses pile up, or when you want to take some time off to pursue a dream or special project. Without a reserve, you will always be living paycheck to paycheck and your flexibility to make different choices will be limited.

Protect your most important assets. Protect your family nest egg by buying health insurance for all members of your family, even if they are healthy. One serious accident can wipe out years of savings. Also, if there is anyone dependent on your income, you need life insurance. Term insurance purchased from a life insurance firm with a strong financial rating is all you need. Have a will, guardians for your children, as well as an "advance medical directive" in place that tells your doctors the type of care you want if you become unable to speak for yourself.

Make spending decisions based on your values. Spend only on the things that add value and energy to your life. Take some time to figure out what that is and then allocate your spending accordingly. If you value adventure, then allocating money to an adventure trip each year is probably more important than buying a big fancy house in the suburbs. If you value family, then spend your money on quality leisure activities for the family instead of expensive clothes. The choices are endless but the money supply is limited. Choose wisely. When you aren't in control of your finances, it is easy to feel helpless. One of the top priorities in my own life, and one of the things that make me feel most empowered, is the freedom that comes from living by these principles. I am a firm believer that asking for help is essential when honing your financial management skills. There are many ways to educate yourself about money. Books such as Suze Orman's *The 9 Steps to Financial Freedom* are available for those of us who learn best from reading. Tapes and CDs are usually available as well. A wealth of information can be found on a daily basis in the Wall Street Journal or on Web sites such as Quicken.com. Another resource which can be key to improving both your financial wisdom and financial health is a trusted financial advisor. Well-planned financial management is an essential life skill if one is to attain financial freedom, achieve success, and have the ability to create the life you want to live.

ENJOY YOUR LIFE WITH WHAT YOU HAVE

If all of this information on managing finances doesn't seem very appropriate, since money is a little scarce right now, here is another perspective. Try to change your focus from what you don't have to what you do have. Perhaps it is time for all of us to make a healthy shift from wanting to valuing what we have. The benefit of the shaky economy of 2009 and 2010 may prove to be the fact that more people are investing in relationships rather than new clothes, dining out, and sporty cars. In the last year or so, many families are finding some pleasant rewards in getting back to the basics in terms of lifestyle. People are thinking more about their priorities, and spending their money accordingly. For instance, if family togetherness is a priority, family picnics or walks on the beach become pleasant substitutes for eating out. You may also have more time to spend with your family—a welcome respite from the non-stop work you may have been caught up in previously. Many of my friends and I spend considerably more time enjoying walking our dogs, and sharing pizza in our homes than ever before—and we're having a great time. I also find that I enjoy spending more time on the phone talking with my children who live in St. Louis, Atlanta, and Baltimore. Quite honestly, I've never felt a stronger connection or more gratitude for friends and family than I do now. There has never been a better time to practice acts of kindness than right now.

Studies have shown that when we give to others—even just a smile—we produce chemicals in our bodies that result in greater tranquility, joy and trust. No matter who you are, or where you fall on the socio-economic scale, it always puts your problems in perspective when you focus on making the day a little brighter for someone whose needs are much greater than yours. This is also a good time to regroup, and remember, once again, the many things that each and every one of us has to feel grateful for. An attitude of gratitude goes a long way toward creating and maintaining a mindset of happiness. When it comes right down to it, and we look around us at those we love, and those things that bring us the greatest joy, maybe the best things in life really are free.

ACTION STEPS:

Many suggestions have been made throughout this chapter for actions that you can take to enhance the level of happiness that you experience in your life. Below is a quick summation of skills that will serve you well in important areas of your life:

1. **Keep your thoughts aligned with the happiness you desire:** As you go through each day, notice your thoughts (your self-talk) about the events of your life. Your emotions (guilt, fear, sadness, anxiety, etc) will let you know when your thoughts are taking you away from happiness. Practice making the shift from focusing on what you dislike in your life to thoughts that are more aligned with what you do like and intend to attract into your life.

2. **Take responsibility for your role in creating happiness in relationships:** Be aware of the communication style you use and whether it is helpful or harmful in your relationships. If needed, practice the skills that you need to communicate assertively on a more consistent basis. Create quality time for communication, and remember the 5 to 1 rule—five positive interactions for every negative interaction.

3. **Nurture your social relationships:** Social support is one of the greatest happiness builders and buffers against stress. Strengthen your social relationships by:

   • making time for your friends,

   • building intimacy through sharing information,

   • demonstrating loyalty and support, and

   • hugging a lot!

4. **Practice effective coping skills when faced with stress and adversity:** Whether problem-focused coping or emotion-focused coping is appropriate for your situation, you need specific skills to maintain the level of happiness you desire. In situations over which you have some control, try making a plan to resolve the problem and acting on it. In other situations, when you have little or no control over the stressful situation, you can try strategies such as:

   • distraction,

   • seeking the support of friends and family,

   • reframing the problem, and/or

   • looking for the benefit in your challenging situation.

5. Keep your energy fuel tank filled: Maintaining a high level of energy is of great importance when your desire is to be at your best and happiest. It is important to be aware of things that drain your energy and things that fuel

your energy. Check the energy draining items below that apply to you (add others if you wish). Review the results of this check list, prioritize items that need some work, and consider which of them you wish to address at the present time. Prioritize your list, and start taking action.

____ There are many people in my life who continuously drain my energy.

____ In my home, I have things that need to be repaired.

____ My home and/or office environment is cluttered.

____ I rarely exercise.

____ I eat food that isn't good for me.

____ My work is stressful and I am exhausted at the end of the day.

____ I have given little thought to my spending habits and the management of my money.

You will also want to build energy boosters into your life. Consider the activities below and check those which you need to incorporate into your life for the purpose of enhancing your energy and your happiness level:

____ Exercise regularly.

____ Maintain healthy eating habits.

____ Spend more time with friends.

____ Clean up the clutter at home and at work.

____ Cultivate healthy relationships (social and romantic).

____ Become skilled at saying "no."

____ Establish boundaries where needed.

6. **Take responsibility for setting goals:** The most satisfying, happiest lives are those filled with meaningful goals that help you focus on what is important to you. Goals provide you with clarity about the things you want, and provide you with a sense of direction for achieving them. Talking about

your goals with others is a good idea since it further motivates you, and helps you attract the right people and circumstances into your life to make the attainment of the goals a reality.

**IF YOU ARE JUST BEGINNING TO SET LIFE GOALS,
HERE ARE SOME IDEAS TO GET YOU STARTED:**

1. Review your values, vision and your mission statement. (This is the work you did in Chapter 7.)

2. Write down some long-term goals that reflect your values and mission:

   - What are your long-term career goals?

   - What are your goals around personal relationships?

   - What "statement" do you want to make with your life (your legacy, how you want to be remembered).

3. Select some mid-term goals that will help you achieve the long range goals identified above (i.e. education or experiences you will need to achieve long-range goals).

4. Now think about short-term goals (things you accomplish in a year or less such as specific courses you need to take, goals with dollar amounts, personal action required to achieve your mid-term and long-term goals.

**IF YOU ARE SETTING GOALS LATER IN LIFE,
HERE IS A SLIGHTLY DIFFERENT VERSION OF
GOAL-SETTING THAT MAY BE OF VALUE TO YOU:**

1. Identify your values and your mission for the rest of your life. (See defining your mission in the exercise above). What do you want your legacy (how you will be remembered) to be? For example, I hope to be remembered as an inspiration to others. This step creates the desire, the motivation.

2. Identify specific measureable goals that are consistent with your mission which you can begin pursuing right away. Each goal provides the motivation and direction you need to keep moving toward your larger life mission.

3. Decide how you wish to carry out the achievement of your goals. You will want to choose a venue that is appropriate to your life purpose. With the achievement of each goal, you will gain confidence and self-esteem.

4. Make the decision that nothing will distract you from your purpose. With a strong desire and persistence, the achievement of your goals is sure to follow.

5. Since you will want to maintain your enthusiasm and involvement in pursuing your dreams, it is a good idea, as you near the completion of one major goal, begin identifying the next goal you wish to achieve. Your goals build on one another to form the foundation for living a purposeful life.

7. Take responsibility for your finances:

   A. Take responsibility for your attitude: To have more, you have to begin thinking you can have more. Notice the words you choose about money. Take a look at the statements below, and see whether or not they are true for you. Those that you mark true indicate that you are leaning toward an abundance mentality. Those that you mark false may represent areas that need work. Just giving thought to your answers to these questions is a good start toward making any necessary shifts in your attitudes about money.

   I believe that if we learn to work together, we can enjoy a world in which there is truly enough for everybody.

   ☐ True   ☐ False

   With appropriate financial advice, managing my money can be an opportunity for personal growth.

   ☐ True   ☐ False

   I feel positive that I can learn what I need to get my finances in order.

   ☐ True   ☐ False

   I am proactive in planning my financial future.

   ☐ True   ☐ False

I contribute to causes that are important to me.

     ☐ True   ☐ False

I am optimistic about my ability to increase my sense of financial well-being.

     ☐ True   ☐ False

B. Take responsibility for your money. Taking charge of your money begins with these important action steps:

- Determine how much income you have,

- Determine how much you spend,

- Create a budget,

- Live within your means,

- Start building a financial reserve as soon as possible.

Why wait? Be happy now!

*In other words, taking care of yourself first allows you
to better take care of others. This wisdom even held true while
I was serving as a care-giver for my husband, Charles.
If I didnt take care of myself through diet, exercise,
rest and even emotional and spiritual self-care.
I didnt have the energy or the attitude to be of help to him.*

CHAPTER 10

The Wisdom of Putting Yourself First

In a time when you barely are able to keep your head above water as you juggle all the demands of a fast paced life, the thought of putting yourself first probably sounds ludicrous. You may find yourself saying, "I don't have time for things like exercising or relaxing. I have a business to run and a family to take care of! There's barely time to take care of everyone else in my life, let alone trying to figure out when to take care of me!" Take a moment to consider this idea: You don't have time not to take care of you by including self-care in your daily life. A major part of living a happy, healthy, productive life is recognizing the needs of your mind, body, and spirit and then taking the steps to meet those needs.

When a life coach first presented the concept of putting myself first, my immediate reaction was, "But that sounds so selfish!" The simple, yet profound, explanation I was given laid to rest any concerns I had. She said,

"When preparing to fly, you are told that in case of an emergency, you should place the oxygen mask on your own face first. Then you will be able to assist children with their oxygen masks, and any other needs they might have." It is not that you consider yourself more important than others. It is about being the best that you can for others. Now, many years later, I found that this wisdom held true while taking care of Charles during his illness. If I had not taken care of myself through diet, exercise, rest, and emotional and spiritual self-care, I wouldn't have had the energy or the attitude that I needed to be of help to him.

In the words of life coach Cheryl Richardson, "A high quality life starts with a high quality you." It is in developing a lifestyle of self-care that you renew your mind and your body on a regular basis, strengthen your resilience, and enhance your personal and professional effectiveness. In order to do that, it is essential to have the knowledge and the tools you need to develop implement the self-care practices that will support not only success in reaching your goals, but your physiological, psychological, and spiritual well-being as well.

A MIND/BODY/SPIRIT MODEL

When I think of all of the factors involved in health and well-being, I think in terms of the mind/body/spirit model. The term mind/body/spirit is used to describe the many complicated interactions that take place among your thoughts, your body, your spirit, and the outside world. Your health and sense of well-being depend on a multitude of factors including genetics, your health habits and lifestyle, your emotional state, your social supports, and your spiritual well-being. You are likely to achieve benefits from positive changes that you make in any one of these areas, but the best results are usually achieved when you address all of them.

A lifestyle of self-care refers to the many things you can do in your daily life that improve your health and well-being. In addition to regular medical care, some of the most important are:

- practicing relaxation on a regular basis,
- exercising regularly,
- maintaining a healthy diet,
- developing social support, and
- connecting with your spiritual nature.

THE IMPORTANCE OF RELAXATION

The chronic stress of our hectic lifestyles results in many harmful effects on your health and well-being, as well as your ability to be productive and effective, it is important to find ways to control and neutralize these effects. One of the things you can do is become aware of the importance of relaxing your mind and your body, and practicing relaxation on a regular basis. Relaxation is your body's built-in mechanism for reversing the damaging physiological effects of stress.

The greatest teachers in many religious traditions have long valued the importance of relaxation and a quiet mind. It is believed that a quiet mind is what allows us to best connect with our own inner wisdom. More recently, researchers have found that when you quiet your mind for as little as fifteen to twenty minutes, even if it is only three or four days a week, positive physiological effects occur in your body. Dr. Herbert Benson, Director of the Mind/Body Medical Institute in Boston refers to these effects as the body's Relaxation Response. This response includes a decreased heart rate and lowered blood pressure, both of which helps us counteract the negative effects of daily stress that result in health problems such as strokes and heart attacks.

As a person who has struggled with high blood pressure, I can personally attest to the value of consciously quieting your mind and relaxing your body. I was placed on blood pressure medication shortly before learning how to consciously relax. As I began practicing relaxation techniques, I was able to discontinue the medication (under the supervision of a physician) and maintain healthy blood pressure levels. But decreased blood pressure wasn't my only benefit. As I learned to relax, I felt much lighter in spirit, and life began feeling joyous rather than burdensome!

In order to achieve the maximum results from relaxation, you may need to learn specific techniques that help you relax and "let go" more easily. Relaxing and letting go physically involves releasing muscles from habitual tension, breathing slowly and regularly, and using the exhalation of your breath to release tension. Letting go emotionally means cultivating an attitude of calmness and composure. Mentally letting go means observing and releasing troubling, worrisome thoughts. Letting go and consciously relaxing on a daily basis is a great benefit, both physically and mentally. While you can't always do away with the stress in your life, you can allow yourself to relax and renew by quieting your mind. In doing this, you relieve tension and anxiety, and allow your body to start the healing process. Deep belly breathing is a great stress management tool and a skill that is helpful when you want to practice relaxation. Many of us aren't aware of the important role that the breath plays in relaxation. When you breathe in, you provide your body with oxygen, which is used to produce energy. When you breathe out, you release the carbon dioxide which is produced in this process.

The regular practice of meditation as a means of relaxation is also thought to contribute significantly to a state of happiness by cultivating awareness and the quality of detachment. There are many kinds of meditation (see Chapter Fifteen) such as concentrative meditation, mindfulness, contemplative, and loving kindness meditations.

If you live with constant stress, your goal may be to simply try to relax your mind and body, and achieve a reversal of the damaged caused from the constant barrage of stressful thoughts and the accompanying release of chemicals that prepare our bodies to fight or flee (the fight-or-flight response). If that is the case, Dr. Benson offers an especially user-friendly meditation technique called the Respiratory One which is described in the Action Steps of Chapter Sixteen.

In addition to conscious relaxation through meditation and other strategies, consider the possibilities for simply learning to live in a more relaxed way. In our work-centered culture, many of us believe that "our life is our work," only to wake up one day wishing that we had spent more time with those we love (including our four-legged companions). I had a big dose of that "wake up" experience when I was pushing myself to complete this book on the schedule I had created in my mind. I found myself retreating to my home office more and more in order to get one more paragraph, one more page, one more chapter written. Before I knew it, I was forgetting to take time out to relax and play. I had severely short-changed my time with my family, my friends, and most noticeably, my dog. I'm embarrassed to say that I was approaching life using the "I'll be happy when" model. "I'll be happy when I finish my book." Fortunately, I quickly realized that happiness isn't achieved by writing a book. Happiness is achieved to the extent that I live fully and with enjoyment of each and every moment including when I'm writing a book. This doesn't mean that I don't enjoy working. I do—very much! But I enjoy it more, and am more productive, when I work, play, take time for self-care, and enjoy the simple pleasures that life has to offer.

REGULAR EXERCISE—AN EFFECTIVE HAPPINESS BOOSTER

You may find that just reading the word "exercise" makes you shudder. The fact is, however, that lack of physical movement and lack of fresh air are closely linked to stress and exhaustion. Good exercise fuels your body, mind and spirit, and is an excellent means of gaining some control over the negative effects of adversity and chronic stress.

People who are resilient tend to exercise on a regular basis. When your body is in a "fight-or-flight" state of arousal, exercise provides a natural outlet and allows the body to return to its normal equilibrium by releasing natural chemicals that build up during stress. Appropriate exercise has been found to:

- minimize the risk of heart attack, diabetes, cancer and hypertension,

- increase good (HDL) cholesterol,

- promote weight control,

- increase quality of life,

- improve sleep,

- protect us from cognitive impairment as we age, and increase longevity.

In fact, surveys have shown that exercise may well be the most effective, instant happiness booster of all activities.

The daily activity that I simply will never miss (barring medical emergencies) is my morning walk with my dog, Abby. Just by getting out and exercising, I notice that my mood brightens, I feel a sense of pride in myself, I enjoy the opportunity to be with friends, I am able to keep a handle on my weight, and—the best part of all—I get a lot of grateful doggie kisses (a wonderful source of pet therapy!).

MAINTAIN A HEALTHY DIET

Although my children accuse me of only eating for survival, I am well aware that a high quality life and a high quality you includes finding a healthy balance of essential nutrients and caloric intake. Good eating habits contribute to a healthy body, and can help prevent or control high blood pressure, heart disease, indigestion, constipation, hypoglycemia, diabetes and obesity. Healthy eating has also been found to reduce irritability, headaches and fatigue (pretty important stuff when it comes to happiness!).

One of the challenges we face in our culture, however, and certain other cultures, is that we eat to celebrate, we eat for comfort, we even eat to observe passages of life. Meals provide an opportunity to relax and socialize and can often help to reduce stress. Unfortunately, we often fail to choose food that is nutritionally sound.

Moderation is the building block of sound nutrition and a healthy diet. It is so tempting to eat too much red meat, poultry with the skin, regular cheese, ice cream and other whole milk dairy products, and fried food. The result is that we often fail to choose enough fruits, vegetables, legumes (beans, lentils, and peas) and whole grain products.

The good news is that there are numerous resources that provide excellent suggestions and guidelines for creating and maintaining a healthy diet. The most basic resource is the Food Guide Pyramid, which provides an outline of what to eat each day based on the Pyramid dietary guidelines. It's not a rigid prescription but a general guide that lets you choose a healthful diet that will help you get the nutrients you need, and at the same time the right amount of calories to maintain healthy weight.

If you are struggling with a weight problem, you may want to enlist the support of friends, family, co-workers, or a group that meets on a regular basis such as Weight Watchers. With their support, the whole process of a weight loss program seems easier, and you are more likely to stick with it. Also, you might consider finding a nutritionist who will partner with you and help you learn what foods you should eat and what foods to avoid. Having someone who can advise you, and to whom you are accountable is a definite plus when trying to achieve weight loss goals. It is an added benefit if your nutritionist is skilled in the psychological/emotional issues that are often connected with food.

THE JOY OF SOCIAL SUPPORT

Have you ever noticed how much better you feel when you can talk about a troublesome situation with a friend? Stress studies have repeatedly shown that the greatest buffer against stress is social support. Happiness studies are also validating the importance of social connections. Researchers are finding that the causal relationship between friendship and happiness appears to be a two-way street. Romantic partners and friends tend to make us happy. And when we are happy, we tend to be more likely to attract friends and lovers.

There may be no better coping mechanism than sharing a problem with a trusted friend. When you have social support you feel cared about, valued, and have a sense of belonging. You have access to advice and guidance, and sometimes even physical or material assistance. In addition to these benefits, there are also health benefits. When people have a healthy social support network, they tend to feel a sense of well-being and a greater sense of control.

Researchers believe that the sense of well-being and control that accompanies healthy social ties acts as a buffer against stress by protecting people from the diseases that stress often causes. Just as feeling isolated has been shown to be detrimental to health, a feeling of connectedness has been shown in repeated studies to be healing. People with strong social support tend to be healthier and live longer. In an analysis of three communities of long living people, (the Sardinians in Italy, Okinawans in Japan, and Seventh-Day Adventists in Loma Linda, California) reveal that the top two things these people had in common were: 1) They put family first, and 2) They kept socially engaged.

I never fully appreciated the richness that friends I interact with on a daily basis could bring to my life until I retired. When I started meeting people as I walked Abby each morning, I was delighted to find that they tended to walk at the same time each day that I did. Over the years, my "dog friends" have become a mainstay of my life, my health, and my happiness. I have discovered that the comfort of another human being may be one of nature's most powerful antidotes to stress. Dr. James Lynch, a well-known researcher in the field of social support, sums up his results as follows: "The mandate to love your neighbor as you love yourself„ is not just a moral mandate. It is a physiological mandate. Caring is biological. One thing you get from caring for others is that you're not lonely; and the more connected you are to life, the healthier you are."

TAP INTO YOUR SPIRITUAL NATURE

There are many ways to tap into the benefits of your spiritual life to increase the amount of happiness and joy in your life. Spirituality means different things to different people. Some think of spirituality as being at peace with self and environment. Others think of spirituality as being in touch with a power greater than oneself. Others equate spirituality with having a sense of purpose, or finding meaning and wisdom in here-and-now difficulties, or enjoying the process of growth and having a vision of one's potential.

The definition of spirituality that resonates most with me is "a search for the sacred"—a search for meaning in life through something larger than the individual self. I see this search expressed as people come together with a goal of helping others. I see it expressed as people engage in random (or not so random) acts of kindness. I see it expressed when we honor ourselves, one another, and this planet for which we are stewards. I see it honored when we choose cooperation rather than competitiveness. I see it honored when we choose laughter over fear, peace over war. If you would like a spiritual boost, listen to the beautiful song, *I Choose Love* by Shawn Gallaway as it reminds us of the power of our choices in shaping our future on our troubled Earth. As I look around at friends and acquaintances, it doesn't come as a surprise that research shows that spiritual people are considerably happier than non-spiritual people.

Being in touch with your spiritual nature and cultivating a spiritual practice doesn't require that you attend a church or temple. Many people search for the sacred through meditation practices in their homes. Others experience being in the presence of God when they are in natural settings such as a woods or on a beach by the ocean.

I find that, in my own life, one of my greatest desires is to feel that spiritual connection to my inner being—my soul—my deepest source of wisdom—my authentic self. I believe that the most fundamental way to honor your spiritual well-being is to listen to the wisdom of your soul, and live your life based on those inner truths. I don't actually hear words of advice, but I do pay attention when my gut instinct is telling me that something isn't in my best interest, and

I usually take action when something "just feels right" to me. It has been my experience that life flows more smoothly when I listen to my inner wisdom on matters of relationships, business decisions, or just finding direction for my life. When I am "tuned in," things just seem to fall in place.

Connecting with your spiritual nature also means reaching deep within yourself to understand the core of who you are. The first step is getting in touch with what gives your life meaning and purpose. The second is recommitting to it frequently. That meaning may lie in family relationships, or humanitarian efforts, or simply taking care of a plant. Whatever you choose, it can serve as a powerful way to feel connected with your Divine nature—that part of you that brings you the greatest joy.

The message on philosopher Peter Russell's answering machine—"Who are you and what do you want"—reminds each of us to ask ourselves those very questions: "Who am I and what do I want?" When you ask yourself those two simple questions on a regular basis, you will find that you easily begin to connect with your spiritual nature, with what is deeply important to you, and with what gives your life meaning and purpose.

CHECK IT OUT

Check out your life as you are living it right now. Do you have the quality in your life that you desire? Are you the quality you desire? When you live a lifestyle of self-care you empower yourself to be the best you that you can be. Instead of allowing yourself to be victimized by the "rat race" that so many of us get caught up in, step back and take time for you. Enjoy your fullest, richest life by living each day from a core value of mental, physical, and spiritual well-being. In honoring yourself and your own needs, you are giving the greatest gift possible to yourself and to others.

ACTION STEPS:

1. **Relaxation:** If you are wanting to quiet your mind and body, and enjoy a state of physiological and mental rest, try this "Respiratory One" meditation technique developed by Herbert Benson, M.D.
   - Sit quietly in a comfortable position with your eyes closed.

- Deeply relax all your muscles. It sometimes helps to tense and then release them starting with your feet and legs and working upward.
- Breathe in deeply through your nose and be aware of your breath.
- Say the word "one" silently while exhaling.

Note: Dr. Benson suggests that you use the word "one" for every breath, rather than trying to count your breaths, losing track, and becoming stressed.

2. **Exercise**: When you are starting an exercise program, maximum well-being is your goal. Be sure to consult with your doctor before starting any exercise program. There are many types of exercise that you might choose, including working out in a gym, jogging, walking, cycling, swimming, dancing, tennis, weight lifting, sit ups, push ups and Pilates, to name a few. I would suggest that you don't work out every day initially. Instead, a great beginning expectation might be three times a week. The long term goal is to establish an exercise program that works for you. Don't forget, it's helpful to have a buddy to exercise with you. Not only will he or she make the walk, swim or sit-ups more fun, that person will hold you accountable. If you can join an established group, that might be a good option. Not only will your fun and consistency increase, but you'll probably make some new friends too.

3. **Healthy Diet:** When life seems incredibly stressful, many of us find it tempting to try to reduce our stress level by eating. While we may get temporary satisfaction from eating, we often pay a high price for this relief, including weight gain and lowered self-esteem. Here are some suggestions if you are needing to implement healthier eating habits

- Find a partner or, better yet, a nutritionist, who will motivate you and help you find a personal way of eating that serves your body best.
- Identify and start eliminating your negative eating habits such as eating snacks or pastries when in a hurry, drinking coffee throughout the day to "keep going," frequently eating fast foods, renewing energy in the afternoon with sugary snacks, rewarding yourself with high calorie snacks in the evening, etc.
- If you are eating in response to stress, consider making changes such as starting the day with a nutritious breakfast, keeping healthy snacks available, eating more fruits and vegetables, drinking lots of water to reduce snacking, cutting

down on caffeine, soft drinks and chocolate, prepare nutritious lunches and "brown bag" it if you work outside the home, make rich meals and desserts a treat rather than a daily habit.

4. **Social Support:** Build and nurture your social support system. Deep, meaningful friendships don't happen by accident. They are made. They are nurtured. Here are some strategies for building and sustaining healthy friendships:

- Take time for other people. Let them know you are interested in them, and create times to get together on a regular basis.

- Affirm your friends' successes. Be supportive in times of need.

- Don't forget to hug—a lot! I love it when my ninety-six year old friend, Sylvia, comes outside as my dog friends and I pass her house with our dogs just to collect some of the morning hugs that energize all of us as we are starting our day.

5. **Spirituality:** There are many ways to tap into the benefits of your spiritual life to increase the amount of happiness and joy in your life. How will you honor your spiritual well-being? Here are some suggestions:

- Set aside regular time, preferably daily, for doing those things which bring you in close alignment with your spiritual nature. It might be participation in a spiritual gathering. It might be a walk in nature. It might be, as in my case, a daily practice of sitting in meditation practicing gratitude and visualizing in detail each aspect of my life as I want it to be, including the spiritual self that I want to be—my highest self. I so enjoy the twenty minutes or so that I set aside at the beginning of each day to light a candle, play inspirational music, close my eyes, and sit in silent meditation—a beautiful way to get each day off to the best start possible.

- Seek out things that bring meaning and purpose to your life. This may mean making contributions to a charitable organization whose mission is in alignment with those things you consider important, or it may mean simply practicing acts of kindness on a regular basis.

- See the sacred in daily life events. As you develop the ability to see holiness in everyday things, and in one another, your sense of gratitude, appreciation, and joy in life will expand on a daily basis.

Donna Daisy

PART 2

Tuning Your Heart to Love

INTRODUCTION

By now, you have a pretty clear understanding of the major role played by your thoughts in determining whether you are living above or below the line on the emotional scale. You have learned how to live with great awareness of how your thinking impacts how you are feeling. You know that if you are feeling sad, angry, guilty, or worried, it's time to do a self-scan and check out your self-talk. (What are you telling yourself about what is going on in your life?)

You know that below the line emotions are directly linked to below the line thinking—negative, pessimistic, judgmental thinking that undermines confidence, self-esteem and happiness. You've learned the importance of having a clear vision, a picture in your head of what you want your life to be all about—what will bring you joy—what will give your life meaning—what will make you bubble with excitement about the things you want to be, do and have in your life. You have learned many skills to enhance confidence and personal effectiveness, and you have learned the critical importance of taking time for your own self-care.

Now, in Part II, we are shifting gears a little. We're getting you out of your head and into your heart. Just as you can train your mind for happiness, you can also tune your heart to love. I'm not speaking of romantic love (although that is delightful, as well.) I am speaking of feelings of love that make your heart swell with joy when you take the time to feel gratitude—gratitude for family, for friends, for pets, for a day of sunshine, for a peaceful heart. Or when you feel optimism, and make a practice of looking on the bright side of things. Or when you practice acts of kindness that bring unexpected joy into someone else's life. Or when you learn that forgiveness benefits the one who forgives more than the one forgiven. Or when you learn the delight of quieting your mind, and going to that sacred space within you of peace and inner wisdom. Or when you simply open your heart in love to a pet who is sharing this life with you.

Our world is undergoing so many changes. We are watching old ways of doing things go by the wayside, and seeing a shift to a new way of life that requires a new mindset and a new way of living. This is a time of opportunity. It is a time that we can move away from the feelings of fear, lack and competitiveness. Instead, we can tune our hearts to love. We can make compassion, gratitude, optimism, kindness, forgiveness, cooperation and love the foundation from which we make powerful changes, not only in our own lives, but in all the world as well. That is my dream. Perhaps it is yours, too.

*There is another nice little fringe benefit of love that
many of us concerned about the effects of increasing age
on our health and appearance will be glad to know.
It appears that love actually makes you look and feel younger.*

CHAPTER 11

Tune Your Heart to Love

There is another factor that has a tremendous potential when it comes to "being happy now." That factor is love. All of us know that loving and being loved is a wonderful and exciting experience. Research, however, is now showing that the benefits of love aren't restricted to romance. As it turns out, love is a very effective "medicine."

The research of Dean Ornish, M.D. has shown that when you feel loved, nurtured, cared for, supported and intimate, you are much more likely to be happier and healthier, and are at a much lower risk of getting sick. What we are learning now, however, is that studies are showing that the person who gives the love also receives significant health benefits.

Feelings of love play a key role in physical health, emotional health, and happiness. Selfless love, such as caring and regard for the welfare of others, and the outpouring of caring for the victims of natural disasters, has been shown to reduce stress significantly while, at the same time, also increase the immune system. Experiencing loving feelings and extending ourselves on behalf of others, rather than focusing on ourselves and our own concerns, not only improves our mental state and reduces depression, it also improves cooperation, reduces aggression, and appears to be a potential antidote to many of the problems of the world.

There is another nice little fringe benefit of love that many of us concerned about the effects of increasing age on our health and appearance will be glad to know. It appears that love actually makes you look and feel younger. Feelings of love increase production of DHEA (dehydroepiandrosterone, the anti-aging hormone that produces feelings of youth and vitality). The explanation for the increase in youthful appearance is the increase in the endorphins produced in the body when feelings of love are experienced. The endorphins increase blood flow to the skin, keeping it soft and smooth while reducing the development of wrinkles, and creating a healthier glow. Scientists at the Institute of HeartMath Research have developed exercises that will allow a person to stimulate feelings of love at will. Those who have participated in these studies increased their DHEA production by an average of 50 percent after six months, and by an average of 90 percent after nine months. In a separate study of thirty volunteers, DHEA was increased by 100%.

The HeartMath studies hold promise for those suffering from stress, as well. How many of you are experiencing right now in your personal lives some of the greatest health, emotional, economic, relationships, and financial challenges ever? The constant pressure of living in our fast-paced, radically changing world has resulted in stress becoming the number one malady of our time. As a life coach, I often work with clients who are experiencing stress, anxiety and depression to such an extent that is significantly interfering with their happiness levels. While all of us are familiar with some of the major stressors such as financial loss, job loss, illness, injury, or career and lifestyle changes, it is the pressure and tension that we feel in response to the smaller, everyday hassles such as traffic jams and waiting in line that actually do the most damage.

Over time, the effects of chronic stress can become disabling and create numerous physiological and psychological problems. In fact, 90% of all health problems are related to stress. Thus, it goes without saying that all of these issues pose a significant threat to our health happiness and sense of well-being.

A new kind of help seems to be just around the corner with the advent of the HeartMath technology that is being developed to help people reduce stress, create emotional balance, and improve overall health and wellness.

The Institute of HeartMath Research Center bases its work on the concept that it is not the external events or situations that do the harm; it's how you respond to those stressful events. More precisely, it is how you feel about them that determines whether you feel the negative effects of stress, and ultimately take action to relieve the stress. HeartMath takes the position that, "Emotions or feelings have a powerful impact on the human body. Emotions, like frustration, insecurity, and depressing feelings are stressful and inhibit optimal health and relief from stress. On the other hand, positive emotions, like appreciation, care, and love not only feel good, they promote health, performance, and feelings of well-being."

The power of the HeartMath research lies in the fact that they have proven that you can learn how to intentionally shift to a positive emotion. When doing so, your heart rhythms immediately change. When such a change occurs, it creates a favorable cascade of neural, hormonal, and biochemical events that reduce stress and revitalize the entire body. These stress relief effects are both immediate and long lasting.

In short, people can be trained to create more coherence in their bodies. Coherence is a term used by scientists to describe a highly efficient physiological state in which the nervous system, cardiovascular, hormonal and immune systems are working efficiently and harmoniously. It is a state very similar to what athletes experience when they are in what is called, "The Zone."

The entire system is based on heart rhythms. When you experience stressful emotions, such as tension, anxiety, irritation, or anger, your heart rhythm pattern becomes irregular and incoherent which negatively affects health, brain function, performance, and your sense of well-being. When you are experiencing positive emotions, such as appreciation, care, joy or love, your heart rhythm pattern becomes more ordered and coherent. A high coherence level is a state associated with positive emotional attitudes which send signals to the brain that reduce stress, improve brain function, hormonal balance, immune response, coordination, and reaction times. The emWave Personal Stress Reliever, a device about the size of a cell phone, provides the user feedback regarding the degree of coherence found in your heart rhythm patterns and displays changes in real-time on a large tri-colored LED (the coherence level indicator). In this situation, the goal in using emWave is to reduce stress by achieving and sustaining high coherence anytime, anywhere. As your stress diminishes and a higher state of coherence is achieved, feelings of well-being, balance and enhanced energy will increase.

In his *De-Stress Kit for the Changing Times,* Doc Childre, the founder of HeartMath, has some very specific heart-based recommendations for people experiencing a great deal of stress. In a sense, you might say these recommendations are designed to bring the heart from fear to love. In other words, tune the heart to love. Here are a few of those recommendations:

1. Communicate and support one another. People who are going through similar experiences can support one another from the heart, and not just the mind. This helps lift spirits, reduce stress buildup, and offset anxiety overload which could put your health at risk.

2. Re-open your heart connection with people. When you offer kindness and compassion, or volunteer to help others in need, it helps you move through your own anger, fear and despair, and into a more coherent state of caring. While worry and uncertainty increase stress hormones, compassion and caring for others release beneficial hormones that help balance and restore your system.

3. Send heartfelt feelings of appreciation and gratitude to someone or something each day (friends, family members, pets). Appreciative feelings activate the body's biochemical systems that diminish stress and stabilize the psyche.

4. Avoid blame, anger and "doom and gloom" projections about the future. Getting caught up in the drama reduces your intuition, which you need as you navigate the choppy waters of changing times. Dwelling on the downside of your situation causes anxiety and fear to increase. Excessive levels of stress hormones like cortisol and adrenalin are released throughout your body, often resulting in physical symptoms and mental and emotional imbalances.

5. Use heart-focused breathing to generate true feelings of calm and balance while reducing stress and anxiety. As you breathe, imagine your breath passing in and out of your heart area, each breath massaging and relaxing the heart. Think of breathing in calm and compassion. Then breathe that relaxation out into the room around you.

6. Use prayer or meditation to quiet your mind and center your heart. Feeling compassion for yourself or sending appreciative or compassionate feelings to others can have a beneficial effect on the hormonal and immune systems. One practice is to extend the following good wishes silently, first to yourself, and then to others. First to yourself:

- May I be filled with loving-kindness.

- May I be well.

- May I be peaceful and at ease.

- May I be happy.

Now, bring to mind people you care about deeply. Breathe kindness into your heart and send it out again with your out-breath as you repeat:

- May you be filled with loving-kindness.

- May you be well.

- May you be peaceful and at ease.

- May you be happy.

These wishes can then be extended to others, such as friends, family, people with whom you may have had difficulties, and people of your community, your country, and the world.

If you are among the many people experiencing financial loss, job layoff, bankruptcy, mortgage foreclosure, or any other of the dramatic changes our society is undergoing, you will find many helpful strategies for keeping yourself grounded and heart-focused by visiting these websites:

- www.glcoherence.org (membership is free)

- www.heartmath.com (click on "personal use" to learn more about emWave technology)

The main lesson being taught, however, is that we can all come through all of the challenges of our times if we tap into our hearts and focus on loving feelings of compassion and caring, for ourselves and one another.

Perhaps the most exciting of all, at least for me, is the recognition by today's scientists that human emotions can literally speak to the magnetic field of our planet. At a recent conference sponsored by Hay House Publishers, I heard scientist, author and lecturer Gregg Braden describe how strong, collective heart-based emotions have an impact on the magnetic field of our planet. The experience in our body that affects magnetism, is called coherence, a very active focus of care, gratitude, and appreciation. As it turns out, intentionally achieving coherence, with all of our systems working together in our bodies, may have a far wider impact than simply serving as a stress reliever. It is believed that through coherence, we can restore harmony and good will on the earth. When people are in coherence, they are more cooperative, less aggressive, and more willing to work together.

A good place to start is for each of us to learn to focus more on caring for one another, feeling gratitude and appreciation for what we have, and learning to forgive. We can choose to be kinder to each other. We can become more cooperative and learn to work together instead of in competition with each other. We can choose to be more aware of our world and honor the earth in the way we live our lives.

Perhaps in the end, it is the way we live in our everyday world that determines not only our happiness level, but our impact on the world as well. With attitudes of love, optimism, gratitude, kindness, compassion for others, and forgiveness, not only are we happier, we are a gift to those around us as well. I believe that as we train our minds for happiness, we can easily tune our hearts to love. In the words of Jo Dunning, spiritual teacher and healer, "Love is the network which weaves our world together. It connects each of us with all of life."

I want to share with you the thought-provoking words to a song that has deeply touched my heart and my personal life choices. The song, *I Choose Love,* was written and performed by artist and musician Shawn Gallaway to address global healing and restoration. Perhaps, as we are making the choice to train our hearts for happiness and tune our hearts to love, we will find ourselves to be a positive, powerful and much needed force as we strengthen and support one another in the new world that is quickly emerging.

I CHOOSE LOVE

(Shawn Gallaway)

I can see laughter, or I can see tears
I see a choice, love or fear
What do you choose?
I can see peace, or I can see war
I can see sunshine, or I can see a storm
What do you choose?

Now I choose to live with freedom flying
From my heart, where the light keeps shining
I choose to feel the whole world crying
For the strength that we can rise above
I choose Love
I choose Love

I can see sharing, or I can see greed
I can see caring, or poverty
What do you choose?
I can see gardens, or I can see bombs
I can see life, or death
Coming on strong
What do you choose?

Now I choose...

I see us healing, the darkness dying
I see us dawning, as one world united
So what do you choose?
Love or fear
Oh, we choose

Now I choose to live with freedom flying
From my heart, where the light keeps shining
I choose to feel the whole world crying
I choose to feel one voice rising
I choose to feel us all united
In the strength that we can rise above
I choose Love
I choose Love
Oh, I choose Love

The words to this song have been reprinted with Shawn Gallaway's permission. 2003 Shrabuvu Music (SESAC)

You can see the video and hear this song that touched my soul by going to Shawn's website, www.shawngallaway.com, and, in the left margin, click on "ICL Video."

ACTION STEPS:

1. In order to start experiencing the feelings of love and caring that produce coherence, try this: When you get up each morning, actually seek out ways to help other people. If all of us would do just this one thing, not only would we feel happier, can you imagine the effect we would have on the world? Pretty powerful stuff for such little cost and effort.

2. While driving down the road, or standing in a grocery line, or any time at all, practice coherence by sending out compassion and care. You can use this compassion meditation:

> May you be filled with loving-kindness.
> May you be well.
> May you be peaceful and at ease.
> May you be happy.

or simply think of things for which you feel appreciation and gratitude.

3. Visit www.glcoherence.org (membership is free) and www.heartmath.com to learn more about personal coherence and the Global Coherence Initiative.

Why wait? Be happy now!

Grateful thinking promotes the savoring of life
experiences in a way that allows you to maximize your
satisfaction and enjoyment of life as it is right now.
The practice of gratitude has been shown to be a far more effective means
of achieving happiness than seeking it through external sources.

CHAPTER 12

An Attitude of Gratitude

In his book, *The Art of Happiness,* author Howard C. Cutler, M.D., shares the wisdom of the Dalai Lama, whose teachings I have respected and practiced in my own life for a very long time. He speaks of two methods of achieving the inner contentment that leads to true happiness. One is to obtain everything we want and desire. But, of course, that doesn't occur for most of us. The second, more effective method, is not to have what we want, but rather to want and appreciate what we have.

The practice of gratitude can increase happiness by 25%, according to Dr. Robert Emmons, author of the book, *Thanks! How the New Science of Gratitude Can Make You Happier."* Happiness isn't about how much you have. It's about appreciating what you have, even when it doesn't seem like a lot by most standards. People who focus on what they are grateful for experience higher levels of positive emotions, cope more effectively with stress, show increased resilience in the face of trauma induced stress, recover more quickly from illness, and experience greater physical health." That's quite a testimony for the benefits of gratitude! Gratitude is one of the few things that can change people's life in a measurable way. When we approach life with gratitude, we shift our focus from negative to positive, from looking at what isn't working in our lives, to what is positive. A grateful heart does amazing things when it comes to putting life in perspective. It reminds us to focus on what's good, especially when things are difficult. According to researcher, Dr. Martin Seligman, "insufficient appreciation and savoring of good events in your past, and overemphasis on the bad ones are two culprits that undermine serenity, contentment, and satisfaction." Gratitude is about much more than just saying thanks. It is more about being in the present moment, counting your blessings, and appreciating your life. According to Dr. Sonja Lyubomirsky, those who practice gratitude tend to be less depressed, anxious, lonely or envious. Instead, they are likely to be happier, more energetic, more hopeful, and to experience more positive emotions.

When Charles and I first were coming to grips with the reality that he would likely never be rid of the infection and enjoy good health again, people would ask us how we dealt with the depression that was always waiting to move in and set up housekeeping with us. We explained that we did initially experience a period of despair, even depression, but we quickly recognized that if we were to have any happiness and quality of life, we needed to step back from our problems and look for those things for which we were grateful.

We had many blessings in our lives, including living in a wonderful geographical location where the sunshine and warmth of each day helped to keep our spirits up, and allowed him to enjoy a great deal of time on the patio reading the newspaper and visiting with friends. Instead of giving in to the few pangs of jealousy that were sometimes triggered by the many golfers enjoying their game practically in our back yard, he became amazingly skilled at refocusing on those things he was still able to enjoy in his life. A surprising benefit of gratitude is that it can help you deal with stress and trauma by putting a different spin on the stressful event, coming to grips with it, and moving on. Because we knew that our time together was now limited, Charles and I became increasingly grateful for every moment we had together and with our friends. It's hard to feel angry and fearful when your thoughts are filled with appreciation.

Not surprisingly, when people experience traumatic events such as job loss, or a diagnosis of a serious illness, they tend to think more negatively. It is harder for them to see the good that is in their lives. But consciously engaging in the practice of gratitude can have a very uplifting effect on a person, often shifting that person away from self- defeating thoughts into more appreciative ones.

Grateful thinking promotes the savoring of life experiences in a way that allows you to maximize your satisfaction and enjoyment of your life as it is right now. The practice of gratitude has been shown to be a far more effective means of achieving happiness than seeking it through external source (money, possessions, beauty), or (for the most part) through trying to change your circumstances. For example, if you have just lost your job, you aren't likely to immediately be able to change that situation, but focusing on the things that are good in your life goes a long way toward training your mind and shaping a mental outlook that will promotes happiness despite the job loss.

If you are a person who experiences gratitude, you are typically aware of the good things that happen to you, and you take the time to express your thanks. As Dr. Martin Seligman points out, you might be grateful for specific things people do for you, such as the many acts of kindness from my friends during the four years of Charles' illness, or for good deeds and good people in general. You might also feel a sense of gratitude toward impersonal or non-human sources, such as God, nature, and animals. In my own life, I have experienced this kind of gratitude for the therapeutic benefits I have received from my dog, Abby, who has been by my side throughout my husband's illness, and since his death—and I tell her "thank you" many times every day.

This quote by Melody Beattie sums up the benefits of gratitude in a beautiful way:

> *"Gratitude unlocks the fullness of life. It turns what we have into enough and more. It turns denial into acceptance, chaos into order, confusion to clarity. It can turn a meal into a feast, a house into a home, a stranger into a friend. Gratitude makes sense of our past, brings peace for today, and creates vision for tomorrow."*

ACTION STEPS:

Remember, your goal when practicing any of these action steps is to raise your happiness level—your emotional set point—even by just a little bit. As I have said previously, my definition of success in life is not about the wealth you accumulate, but the amount of joy you experience in your life. Once you have decided that nothing is more important than that you feel good, a good place to start is looking for the things that are already in your life that you appreciate.

1. **Notice your feelings.** A good starting point for increasing your happiness level is to first notice how you are feeling. Write down where you would place yourself right now on the Emotional Scale as discussed in Chapter Four. Next, get a pen and paper, and start the process of raising your emotional set point by looking around you at everything in your environment. Start noticing the things that please you, that make you feel good. Write them down. Keep noticing more and more things that please you, and write these down as well. For example, as I am sitting here in my chair, I first notice my dog, Abby, who is lying on the floor beside me. I notice my computer that has been serving me well with little or no repair for the last two or three years. I glance out the window, and enjoy the sun shining on my lawn and flowers. How could life get any better than this? My emotional set point is definitely at contentment, probably higher. You can do this exercise as many times as you want throughout the day. The more things you find to appreciate, the better you feel. And, as I have said before—but it is worth saying again—the better you feel, the better it gets.

2. **Practice expressing gratitude.** Dr. Martin Seligman suggests this exercise when you want to direct your appreciation to a specific person in your life. This is how it is done. Think of an important person from your past to whom you are grateful for making a major, positive difference in your life. Write a testimonial just long enough to cover one laminated page. When you are ready, share it with the person for whom it is written—in person—and not over the phone or by email. Bring a laminated version of your testimonial with you as a gift. Read it aloud slowly, with expression and eye contact, and let the other person react unhurriedly. Spend time talking

about the things that make this person so important to you. I can almost promise you that if you engage in this particular gratitude practice, you cannot fail to experience significant joy, happiness, and increased warmth toward other people in your life.

3. **Nightly gratitude ritual.** This is an effective nightly ritual requiring very little time. Each night when you go to bed, identify and say thanks for something for which you are grateful (good friends, good health, etc). Focus on a new and different object of gratitude each night. While this exercise will be easy at first, you will soon be stretching your mind to find something new for which to give thanks each night. Before long, you will be consciously looking for new things to be grateful for all day long. You will be focusing more and more on things that please you, and less on those things that do not please you. As you become more mindful and give more attention to the blessings in your life, old habits of negativity are gradually replaced by new thoughts of appreciation.

4. **Create a collage.** Consider creating a collage of pictures of things that make you happy (flowers, sunshine, friends, pets). Then display the collage in a place where you can see it and enjoy it every day. The principle is the same as that in the previous exercises—the more you focus on things that make you happy, the higher you move on the emotional scale.

5. **Mealtime gratitude:** Here is a "quickie" that you and your family might enjoy together. When sitting down with your family to eat a meal, take a few minutes to go around the table asking each person to speak and share one thing he or she feels appreciation for.

6. **Visualization.** Here is another "quickie," and one of my personal mood lifters: When you catch yourself slipping into negative thoughts, feelings and behaviors, try, instead, visualizing something that brings you great joy, For me, visualizing the dogs that Abby and I play with every morning as they romp and roll in the grass always evokes a smile and instant feelings of happiness. I find that as I hold my focus on joyous things, I always feel my spirits rising.

7. **Gratitude in tough times:** Remember that when you are at your lowest, and feeling the least thankful, that is when you most need the benefits of gratitude. At the start of your day is a good time to review those things for which you are grateful. These things can be as basic as gratitude for the bed in which you sleep, and a roof over your head. Then your list might expand to include people in your life for whom you are grateful. This starts your day with a fresh perspective that brings with it feelings of hope, peace and happiness. I have noticed that, when I start my day with a clear focus on those things for which I am grateful, I am elevated to a higher place of good feelings, and when I feel good, I attract more good things into my life. Regardless of your circumstances, each day is truly a gift, and gratitude is always the appropriate response to such a gift.

Why wait? Be happy now!

The value to you in all of this is that as you begin to realize that you can deliberately cause even a slight improvement in how you feel, and as you learn to move from depression through anger, through overwhelm and frustration and on up the emotional scale, you have reclaimed your true power to create your life as you want it to be.

CHAPTER 13

The Power of Optimism

"A pessimist is one who makes difficulties of his opportunities.
An optimist is one who makes opportunities of his difficulties."

Francis Bacon

Have you ever had a friend say to you, "Stop thinking so negatively. You need to be more positive!" Most of us have had that experience, and at that moment, we pretty much wanted to shove our friend's well-intended words right back down his or her throat. While you probably "get it" that you are theoretically capable of being more cheerful and upbeat, at that particular moment in time, you simply don't know how to make the leap to the better thoughts and feelings your friend is suggesting.

When you are caught up in negativity, start by taking a look at exactly how you feel. Without fail, your emotions give you very clear feedback about your current level of happiness. Let's say that something has happened that is making you feel terrible. Perhaps you are feeling fear, guilt, anger, or pessimism or even depression. You would much prefer to be experiencing feelings of contentment, hopefulness, optimism, enthusiasm, and love of life, but where do you start? What will get you unstuck, and help you start raising your happiness level?.

The answer is so simple as to be deceptive. The solution lies in finding a thought, any thought, that makes you feel better. As you become consciously aware of how each thought feels, you can begin to guide your thinking in a way that allows you to move up the emotional scale to a higher level of happiness. So the process is that you think a thought and then evaluate how that thought makes you feel. You are looking for thoughts that initially give you relief, and gradually move you upward toward an increased appreciation of life.

You may not be able to move into what I call the above the line feelings right away, but what you will notice is that just moving from depression to anger is an improvement in how you feel. If you are angry, you don't feel as helpless, as trapped, as claustrophobic as you did when you felt depressed. You actually feel slightly better. So you look for thoughts that feel even just a little bit better, and a little bit better. You're making progress. You have consciously chosen an angry thought because it feels better than a thought of hopelessness. You are starting to feel a little sense of control. Now you might look for a thought that brings you upward on the emotional scale from anger to, perhaps, disappointment. That feels even better—not good yet—but better than anger, and certainly better than depression and despair.

A word of advice, don't become overly concerned about the labels I am giving to your many emotions. The idea is simply that you keep reaching for thoughts that give you better and better feelings. As you keep adjusting your thoughts in a way that produces an improved feeling level (psychologists call this process reframing), you begin to feel more and more in control over your life (a sense of empowerment, feelings of self-efficacy). You know where you are now with feelings of depression and disempowerment, guilt, anger, overwhelm, disappointment, frustration, and where you want to be which includes hopefulness that a bright future is possible, optimism and enthusiasm about what the future holds, and a sense of empowerment that says "Yes, I can do this!"

The value to you in all of this is that as you begin to realize that you can deliberately cause even a slight improvement in how you feel, as you learn to move from depression through anger, through feeling overwhelmed and frustrated and on up the emotional scale, you have reclaimed your true power to create your life as you want it to be, and as you want it to feel.

Now, here is the challenge. The thoughts you are thinking right now represent a lifetime of accumulating many beliefs and ways of explaining things to yourself (your explanatory style) which may no longer be serving you well. For instance, you just lost your job, and you are telling yourself, "It's all my fault. I'm never going to find another job. I'm such a terrible father. I'll never be able to provide for my family. Our whole life is ruined." If that is the case, you are probably pretty close to despair on the emotional chart. You will only start improving the way you feel when you are able to start changing your self-talk, and finding better, more optimistic thoughts that are believable to you (believable is the key word). With more optimistic thoughts, not only your feelings, but your entire future will be brighter as a result of the positive effects of optimism.

Optimism is defined in the dictionary as 1) the tendency to take the most cheerful view of matters or to expect the best outcome, and 2) the practice of looking on the bright side of things. Pessimism is defined as 1) the tendency to expect misfortune, or the worst outcome in any situation, 2) the practice of looking on the dark side of things. Whether you live your life from optimistic beliefs or pessimistic beliefs is a key determinant in how you will feel at any given time, how well you cope with stress and adversity, and whether you are successful in making your dreams a reality, all of which has a direct impact on your level of happiness.

FIVE REASONS OPTIMISM IS SO POWERFUL
IN YOUR LIFE EXPERIENCE

Research has shown that an optimistic approach to life is a powerful life enhancer, benefitting you in many important ways:

1. It increases the likelihood that you will live a longer, healthier life than those who expect the worst.

2. It increases the likelihood that you will persist in trying to achieve your goals, regardless of any difficulty you come up against.

3. Because optimists are likely to persist, even in the face of adversity, they are more likely to be successful in many areas of life including interpersonal relationships, career, social life, and health, all of which contribute to an increased level of happiness.

4. Optimism provides hope, and is your motivation to engage in active and effective coping activities in times of stress. For example, when my husband became ill, we accepted the reality of the situation, but at the same time, we continuously made efforts to make the best of the situation, and even grow from it. I have often said that the four years I spent as caregiver for Charles were without a doubt my most growth-ful, if not the most rewarding years of my life so far.

5. Optimists tend to have a strong belief in their own ability to handle life's challenges (self-efficacy) and therefore, are less likely to succumb to depression and anxiety when times are tough. They feel a sense of control over their destiny, and are motivated to do whatever it takes to get them through the difficulties they face.

IS OPTIMISM A "HEAD IN THE SAND" APPROACH TO LIFE?

During workshops I have presented, I have noticed that participants sometimes become uncomfortable when I suggest that optimism is a key component of happiness and resilience. They believe that optimism carries with it an implied message that, "You don't have to be accountable or take responsibility for the outcome. Just think positive and everything will be fine." This is definitely not my message. Research has shown that optimists have a clear understanding that the world can be a cruel and dangerous place, or a kind and benevolent place. They just choose which of those two views to put in the foreground of their lives, recognizing all the while that outcomes are usually dependent on their efforts.

While it is important to recognize the reality of your adverse situation, you are far more likely to overcome difficulties in your life and remain happy if you develop the ability to work your way up to a more constructive, more optimistic way of thinking about the challenges you are facing. I tend to be very optimistic, but at the same time, I believe in taking action to achieve the outcomes I want. It is my belief that your strongest course of action in hard times is to first keep a close eye on how your thinking is impacting your feelings and where you are on the emotional scale, since this is a key determinant to how hopeful, enthusiastic, and motivated you are. If you are below the line, it may be time to do some "thought adjustments" to start bringing yourself up the scale to optimism (or higher). Next, make sure that you are taking responsibility for trying to achieve the best possible outcome for the challenging situation.

IS OPTIMISM INNATE OR LEARNED?

Some optimists are born that way. Others attain optimism by learning to recognize the power of their own thinking and training their minds by practicing exercises and strategies that have been proven to work. Because your explanation style (what you tell yourself about the world in general, and your situation in particular) is so important, almost all of the optimism strategies involve finding a more positive way to look at the world, and shining your light on the positive at every opportunity. Changing your thinking patterns so that you can move from pessimism to optimism requires effort since you are building a new habit. You can probably guess that the way to solidify and internalize this new habit is practice, practice, practice.

ACTION STEPS:

There is no doubt that an optimistic outlook on life contributes to happiness, health and well-being. If you are inclined toward pessimism (negative thinking) and notice that it is undermining your confidence, interfering with your performance, and diminishing your mental skills, here are some techniques you can practice to develop new, more positive thinking habits:

1. **Take charge of your thoughts.** Many people believe they have no control over how they feel because they are so often not able to control the circumstances that they believe are making them feel bad. What these

people have forgotten is that is what you think about your circumstances (what you tell yourself, your self-talk) that really determines how you feel. Jerry and Esther Hicks, in their books on the teachings of Abraham, devised an excellent format for practicing the art of changing your thinking in a way that will promote a better feeling state. This exercise is an approximation of that format.

Step 1. When you have had a challenging situation in your life and are feeling stuck in negativity, refer back to the emotional scale in Chapter Four. Identify which feeling on the scale is the closest match to where you are emotionally at the present time.

Situation: _____

Emotion: _____

Step 2. Recognizing that how you feel is directly linked to your thoughts, identify what you are telling yourself about your situation. For example, if you have just lost your job, you might be thinking, "I can't believe I lost my job. I'm such a loser. I'll probably never be able to find another job. My whole life is ruined." Your emotional level is probably beyond pessimism, and fairly close to hopelessness and despair. If, on the other hand, you are telling yourself, "It's devastating to lose a job, but I have a good support system of friends and family, and with their help, I'm sure I can get on track soon. In the meantime, I'm going to enjoy spending more time with family," your emotional level is more likely to be hopeful and optimistic.

Step 3. Remembering that your goal is simply to improve how you feel, try new thoughts. Try making new statements to yourself about your situation that will start gradually moving you up the emotional scale toward optimism or even higher. Your statements to yourself might look something like this:

"I can't believe I lost my job. I'll probably never find another job." (Hopelessness)

"I don't see any way this situation can turn out well." (Pessimism)

"I'm causing such a hardship for my family." (Guilt)

"My boss is so thoughtless. He could have at least told me what was going on." (Blame)

"I wish someone would do this to him—just terminate his job without giving him a clue." (Revenge)

"Getting back out into the world of job seeking is a scary thought." (Overwhelmed)

"I don't even know what a decent looking resume looks like anymore." (Overwhelmed)

"I worked really hard and still lost my job. You can't rely on keeping a job anymore in this economy." (Frustration)

"At least I will get to spend more time with my family." (Hopefulness)

"It will actually feel good to have the opportunity to see what other jobs are out there." (Enthusiasm)

"Maybe I'll even be able to find a job that allows me to have more time with my family." (Optimism, Enthusiasm)

"My wife has been so helpful through all of this." (Appreciation)

"All things considered, things will probably work out just fine. (Optimism)

2. **Best possible selves diary.** This exercise was introduced by Dr. Sonja Lyubomirsky in her book, *The How of Happiness,* and is an excellent exercise for enhancing well-being and optimism about the future. In this exercise, you sit in a quiet place for 20 to 30 minutes and think about what you want your life to be one, five, or ten years from now. Visualize a future for yourself where everything has turned out as you wanted. Writing your responses to this exercise puts in the foreground of your thoughts the possibility of a delightful future, and motivates you to persist in your efforts to achieve your goals. Simply visualizing such a bright future stimulates your desire, motivation and optimism about a future for which you feel great enthusiasm. I do a version of this exercise every morning before dog walking time, as I go over my mental checklist of every key area of my life and what I want it to look like. In this way, I am excited about the future, and eager to do what I need to do to make that future a reality.

3. **Make friends with happy people.** Feelings, good or bad, are contagious. If you want to be happy, make friends with happy people. If you hang out with sad and depressed people, you will likely "catch" their sadness and depression.

4. **Take a break from the media.** Other than the weather channel, I've hardly watched TV for months. I was discovering that between the news about the economy, war, and local muggings, my natural sense of optimism was having a very difficult time staying afloat. With the television turned off, my house is peaceful, my spirits are lighter and it is easier to develop and maintain the positive mindset with which I want to live my daily life.

5. **Go to your "good places."** I keep a few "feel good" scenes in my memory so that if I find I am feeling down in the dumps, I mentally go to my stash of "feel good" visualizations such as dogs romping in the grass, and quickly bring them up on my mental screen, and my day brightens up in a heartbeat!

Please note: If depression and/or anxiety becomes chronic, be sure to see your doctor.

Why wait? Be happy now!

Helping others tends to raise your awareness of your own

blessings in life, and increases feelings of gratitude.

It takes the focus off of you, and places it on those in need.

CHAPTER 14

Little Things Mean a Lot: Practicing Acts of Kindness

Several years ago, I was deeply touched by the movie, "Pay It Forward." The film is the story of an 11 year old boy, Trevor, given a social studies assignment to think of and implement an idea that would change the world. From this challenge, the concept of "pay it forward" is born. The essence of "pay it forward" is that when someone does an act of kindness on your behalf, rather than paying them back, you do something kind for three other people who will, in turn, do something kind for three more people, thus creating a chain of kindness with a ripple effect of goodwill and positive social consequences.

From a very early age, we are taught that kindness and compassion are important virtues. If you are a religious person, you are probably aware that kindness and compassion are at the heart of every great religious tradition.

Interestingly, these activities represent much more than just cultivating feelings of warmth and affection as a means of improving your relationship with other people. They are mental attitudes based on the wish for others to be free of their suffering, along with a sense of commitment, responsibility, and respect for the others.

HOW DO ACTS OF KINDNESS AND COMPASSION FIT INTO OUR EVERYDAY LIVES?

Scientific research has actually demonstrated that increasing kind behaviors is an effective way to increase happiness in your own life. In other words, acts of kindness are not only good for the recipient, but good for the doer as well.

I want to share with you my favorite kindness story, in which I was the recipient of the kindness. When I lost my husband, best friend, and soul mate to a four-year battle with numerous health problems in September, 2009, my heart was broken, and I mostly wanted to be alone. The thought of returning to Greenville, Illinois, where we lived and Charles practiced medicine for 42 years, and spending hours at visitation talking about his death, seemed unbearable.

How wrong I was! An amazing thing happened during the four hours I greeted the endless line of people who came to pay their respects. I quickly realized that it was a great honor to listen to each person's story about how Dr. Daisy had touched his or her life, or that of a family member. Can you imagine a greater act of kindness than that shown by everyone who took their time to be with me on that day? To add to the blessing, my children and grandchildren also got to hear these stories, and the gratitude that these people expressed for Charles' presence in their lives. As it turned out, the four days I spent in Greenville talking with family, friends, and former patients of my husband—laughing at some stories, crying at others—was one of the most uplifting experiences of my life. When I returned to Naples, I came back with a heart filled with inspiration and joy—all due to the kindness and willingness of so many people to share their time and their stories with me.

Another kindness story that I enjoy sharing with others is one which occurred several years ago when I had the opportunity to experience in my own life the "pay it forward" effect. While working as a psychologist, I donated quite a lot of time to an 11 year old boy named Danny, who was referred for truancy and possible drug involvement. At age 12, he was arrested for using and selling drugs, and placed in juvenile detention. I lost track of Danny until ten years later, when I received a call that was one of the highlights of my life. The caller said, "Dr. Daisy, this is Danny. I want to tell you that I'm five years clean and sober, have a good job, attend AA regularly, and I'm working a good program. You believed in me and planted the seeds for a better life. Now I want to spend my life doing the same for young boys struggling like I did."

Helping others satisfies our basic human need to connect with others, and has a positive effect on our emotional and physical health. I love the study by David McClelland, a psychologist at Harvard University, who demonstrated that even when we simply view compassionate acts, we experience an increase in immunoglobulin-A, an antibody that can help fight respiratory infections. (I get my personal immunoglobulin-A fixes by watching re-runs of Steven Spielberg's beautiful movie, *ET: The Extra-Terrestrial*—and it's more fun than taking Vitamin C!)

Other research findings demonstrate that being kind and generous leads you to perceive others more positively and charitably. Kindness has also been shown to promote a greater sense of working together, as well as cooperation in families, communities, and indeed, the world at large.

Helping others tends to raise your awareness of your own blessings in life, and increases feelings of gratitude. It takes the focus off you, and places it on those in need. It also improves your perception of yourself as an altruistic person, raises your self-esteem, and promotes feelings of confidence, optimism, usefulness, and a greater sense of control over your life—all powerful contributors to happiness.

There are many other studies demonstrating the benefits of kindness, but, in the end, we don't need to rely on experiments and surveys to confirm the real value of compassion and acts of kindness. We can witness on a daily basis the close links between a caring, generous spirit, and personal happiness in our own lives and in the lives of those around us.

ACTION STEPS:

We often seek our happiness through the acquisition of bigger homes, faster cars, and more impressive jewelry, but, in the end, maybe that's not what it is all about. What I realized during my trip back to Greenville for the celebration of my husband's life was this simple, yet profound truth: It is the quality of our relationships—the love, compassion, and kindness we show to one another, especially during difficult times—that brings the greatest joy to our lives.

Each of us can find many ways to make the world a nicer, more loving place as we also benefit from the surge of happiness our actions bring to us. There are no specific "how-to's." The key is that your actions come from the heart. Here are some of my favorite ideas for building kindness into your life on a daily basis:

1. **Be a source of kindness.** This is the "practice random acts of kindness" thing. We can spread joy to others through simple acts such as feeding someone's parking meter that was about to expire, or paying a toll for the car behind you, or even just smiling at someone at the grocery store. Tell people when they've done a good job. Say "I love you" to those who mean the most to you. Tell them how special they are to you.

2. **If you receive an unexpected smile, put a smile on your face** as a gift to the next person you see. It's easy; it's free; it's delightful.

3. **Be a good listener.** When I was training to become a therapist and life coach, great emphasis was placed on listening for the emotions behind the words people spoke. Whether we are receiving the loving attention of caregivers when we are babies, or interacting with other people when we are fully grown, we all need to be listened to and responded to. In the words of Dr. Joan Borysenko, "Listening is a powerful form of communication. While the mouth is still, the heart can speak volumes about how much you care."

4. **Each day, tell at least one person one thing you like admire, or appreciate about them.** It is amazing how much you can improve someone's day with this simple gesture.

5. **Increase your awareness of others.** Kindness grows out of noticing the needs of other people and being responsive to them. I have noticed in my own life that the busier I get, the more my awareness suffers, and kindness often takes a back seat to expediency. You may have noticed, too, that as the pressures of your busy life increase, you are more likely to become irritable and pay significantly less attention to others (strangers, people you work with, family and loved ones that we have chosen to spend our lives with). Be mindful. Notice what is going on with others around you, and assist whenever possible and appropriate.

6. **Volunteer.** If you are short of money, give the gift of time. A few years ago, Ram Dass wrote a book called, *How Can I Help*. In this book, he explained that if you truly want inner peace, giving of your time and talents through volunteer work can help achieve it. And, according to researchers, your health and longevity also benefit from these acts of kindness. That sounds like a bargain to me!

7. **Click to give for free.** This is my personal favorite. Go online each day to www.thehungersite.com and www.theanimalrescuesite.com, and click to give free good and care. (You can ask these websites to send daily email reminders.)

Forgiveness implies a sense of control through the exercise of choice,

and the self-discipline to make the choice that will serve you best.

This is very empowering.

CHAPTER 15

Forgive and Forget~Who Me?

Most of us, at one time or another, have been told that we should forgive a person when he or she has wronged us. But the word forgiveness conjures up some highly charged responses. For some, it is a religious mantra that means accepting the core of all human beings as the same as yours, and giving them the gift of not judging them—and incorporating this practice into your daily life. Others tend to bristle at the concept of forgiveness, and think, "I have the right to be angry after what he did to me!" I must confess that I am a recovering "bristler."

I have read enough research to know that anger and resentment are likely to do far more damage to me than to the person with whom I am angry. About the time I was writing this chapter, I happened to see an Oprah episode in which she exposed puppy mills for the horror they really are. I sat and wept, and certainly didn't want to think about forgiveness. Instead, I wanted to do even worse things to those breeders than they were doing to their dogs. Needless to say, this incident forced me to seriously think through the issue of forgiveness and whether or not I would ever be able to "put my money where my mouth (or pen, in this case) is."

WHAT DOES IT MEAN TO FORGIVE, ANYWAY?

I had to do some serious research to get my mind wrapped around this whole concept of forgiveness. Examples of unthinkable behaviors kept coming to mind, accompanied by the obvious question, "How could I possibly forgive that behavior?" If I am wronged or hurt by another person, the reaction I usually have is to want revenge or at least to avoid that person. So, going on the premise that forgiveness is a contributor to happiness and well-being and a skill that I want to strengthen in my own life, I found that I needed to fully understand what researchers and psychologists mean when they promote forgiveness.

WHAT FORGIVENESS IS **NOT**

When you have been wronged, hurt, insulted, betrayed or attacked by another person, there is always a decision to be made. Do I try to avoid that person? Do I seek revenge? Or do I take the higher road of forgiveness? If you are faced with such a decision, it might be helpful to consider what forgiveness is not.

First of all, forgiveness, as used by scientists and psychologists, does not mean that you resume the same relationship with the person who committed the offense. The woman who was sexually abused by her father doesn't have to go to his house for Sunday dinner. Nor is forgiveness pardoning (as in the judicial system) or condoning the behavior by justifying, minimizing or tolerating it. In fact, forgive and forget isn't exactly what is being suggested by the psychologists.

Rather, forgiveness means that you make a choice. You choose to mitigate or suppress your desire for avoidance of the person or revenge, which is almost always accompanied by below the line feelings of anger, disappointment and hostility. What you choose, instead (whether for spiritual reasons or for reasons of personal well-being such as improved mental health and personal well-being), are the above the line emotions that come with not allowing yourself to be preoccupied with the victimizer's act.

WHY SHOULD WE CHOOSE FORGIVENESS?

Forgiveness implies a sense of control through the exercise of choice and the self-discipline to make the choice that will serve you best. This is very empowering. Probably the most profound reason to forgive was spoken by Nelson Mandela when he was asked how he was able to bring himself to forgive his jailers, Mandela replied, "When I walked out of the gate, I knew that if I continued to hate these people, I was still in prison." In other words, forgiveness sets the forgiver free. In addition to scientific research, many religious traditions have shared with us their wisdom about holding on to anger. This one is from the Buddha: "Holding onto anger is like grasping a hot coal with the intent of throwing it at someone else; you are the one getting burned." Forgiveness, on the other hand, is healing. Forgiveness is something you do for yourself, not for the person who has wronged you.

Jesus taught us not to judge so that we, ourselves, will not be judged. Letting go of judgment is another way of defining forgiveness and every bit as challenging. I am still taking baby steps on this one, but hopefully, I will one day grow into my running shoes.

My personal motivation for forgiveness is not a religious or spiritual or moral one. In fact, I could say that it is a selfish one. I consider forgiveness beneficial because research has shown that people who forgive are less likely to be depressed, anxious, angry and neurotic—and one thing I know for sure, I want to avoid those things. My goal is to live consistently above the line, and enjoy the more positive above the line experiences of being happier, healthier, more agreeable, and more serene. Thus, it appears that forgiveness is a more desirable option than anger, and the desire for revenge or avoidance.

I do want to note that there is some disagreement among experts about when forgiveness is or isn't appropriate. I recall a woman with whom I worked who had been gravely mistreated by her husband. It absolutely was not in her best interest to keep returning after disagreements, and maintaining her relationship with her abusive husband. Yet, she explained to me that when he approached her, and wanted to "make up," she always caved in and ended up right back in the abusive situation. As a result, her psychiatrist advised her that in this case, fanning the flames of her anger was a better approach for her than forgiveness. My advice to you is to read this chapter, and then make a personal, well thought out decision regarding whether or not forgiveness is the right path for you.

ACTION STEPS:

If you choose to work on the art of forgiveness in your own life, be gentle with yourself. Remember that learning to forgive is a process. It takes time, maybe a lifetime. But it is a noble and worthwhile endeavor, and certainly a healthy choice for happiness and well-being.

Here are some tips that have been helpful to me as I work on my personal forgiveness skills. As with any advice, take what is helpful, and leave the rest.

1. **Remember** that forgiveness is a conscious decision that will benefit you physically and emotionally. It also helps you take responsibility for your own happiness.

2. **Understand** that as you practice forgiveness, you may first need to work through emotions such as shock, anger, pain, and/or grief.

3. **Accept** that "forgive and forget" is probably an unrealistic ideal. You may never really forget what happened to you, but you can let go of it—and it is the letting go that allows healing.

4. **Avoid** the mindset that forgiveness is a weakness. It takes a stronger person to forgive than to attack.

5. **Don't get discouraged.** Forgiveness isn't for the faint of heart, nor is it easily achieved.

6. **Give yourself a simple challenge.** Identify someone in your life against whom you hold a grudge, and make a choice to forgive him or her. You can do this in person, or only in your mind. In either event, you rid yourself of the harmful physiological and psychological effects of negativity and open yourself to a healthier, happier lifestyle.

7. Repeat number 6.

8. Repeat number 6.

Why wait? Be happy now!

173

You give yourself a great gift , physically and emotionally,

by incorporating meditation into your life on a daily basis.

While you can't always get rid of the problems and stress in your life,

you can allow yourself to relax and renew by quieting your mind.

CHAPTER 16

Meditation: Getting to The Heart of Things

When trying to make the decision about whether in include a chapter on meditation in this book of strategies for happiness, my hesitation wasn't whether I believed meditation to be an important contributor to mental and physical well-being. I have no doubt of that.

My hesitation came from my lack of formal training in meditation techniques, and my complete lack of experience in training with the masters of meditation. On the other hand, if personal experience counts for anything, I have quite a lot to say about meditation.

Early on, I was a foot dragging, "Do I really have to do this?" kind of meditator. I couldn't imagine how I could possibly sit still and clear my mind of thoughts when my "to do" list was a mile long, and my thoughts were continuously racing, jumping around from here to there. What I discovered, however is that the quieting of the mind which is accomplished through meditation is, without a doubt, a key factor in the achievement of genuine and sustainable happiness. And since happiness is at the top of my list of ingredients for a fulfilling, exciting life, count me in on the meditation thing!

We know that the greatest teachers in many religious traditions have long valued the importance of a quiet mind. Many of these teachers believe that by quieting our mind, we are better able to be in touch with God, by whatever definition we put on him, her or it. Some say that a quiet mind allows us to connect with our inner wisdom. More recently, researchers have found that quieting our minds has a significant positive impact on our health. Studies have shown that when we are able to quiet our minds for even as little as 15 to 20 minutes in the morning and again in the evening, there are positive physiological effects that occur in our bodies, as well as psychological effects, including decreased anxiety, less depression, feelings of peacefulness and an increase in feelings of happiness.

WHERE DO I START?

If you are considering implementing meditation practices in your own life, it's easy to get overwhelmed by the many types of meditation such as Zen (which is at the heart of Zen Buddhism and seeks the attainment of enlightenment), Transcendental (derived from Hindu traditions that promote deep relaxation through the use of a mantra), and Vipassana (seeking insight into the nature of reality). There are also many categories such as mindfulness meditation, loving-kindness and compassion meditation, concentrative meditation, and contemplative meditation. But at the heart of all of these traditions is the core ingredient of first emptying your mind of distracting thoughts. Choose a quiet environment, sit comfortably, and focus your attention on your breath as you breathe in and out. When a thought enters your mind, gently let it go, and refocus your attention on your breath. As you do this over a period of time, you gradually train yourself to keep your focus on your breath, with fewer and fewer stray thoughts wandering in to your mind. You will notice as you practice, you are soon better able to achieve and sustain a relaxed state and enjoy the many physiological and emotional benefits.

What differs across the traditions is your attention focus. In contemplative meditation, your focus may be on your breath or on a single word such as "om." In mindfulness meditation, you might focus on an object or sound non-judgmentally. In compassionate meditation, your focus may be on loving wishes for others, with a goal of developing altruistic emotions and behaviors toward all people. In contemplative meditation, your focus might be on connection with your inner wisdom (your soul, God), or on the meaning of life.

THE HEALTH BENEFITS OF MEDITATION

The benefits people look for in their meditation practices are probably as different as the people who do the meditating. My first experience with meditation occurred when I was teaching stress management for a hospital in Greenville, Illinois. Because of my own ongoing bouts with high blood pressure, I was keenly aware of the body's physiological responses to stress, namely the fight-or-flight response. For example, when you come face -to-face with an unwanted situation, whether it is coming upon a bear in the woods or being called on the carpet by your boss, the fight-or-flight response kicks in. Your heart pounds, your blood pressure rises, your muscles tense and your pupils dilate. That response is hardwired into us from the days when people actually did come face to face with bears and tigers and had to make a choice about whether to stay and fight, or run for their life (literally).

Danger presents itself a little differently in our complex, high tech world. It may take the form of unpaid bills, an unhappy marriage or some unwanted situation produced entirely in your imagination. But the perception of danger to your well-being still triggers the fight-or-flight response, which acts the same way in the body as it would if you were faced with a tiger.

If you experience stress on a fairly consistent basis (chronic stress), your body is in fight-or-flight mode most of the time and is continually producing stress hormones. Air traffic controllers probably experience this phenomenon. Research had concluded that chronic stress and the body's consistent production of stress hormones increase the likelihood of health problems, including high blood pressure, ulcers, stroke and heart attacks, to name a few.

My personal goals at that time were centered around the physiological benefits of meditation, which included:

- Decreased blood pressure
- Decreased heart rate
- Decreased breathing rate
- Decreased muscle tension
- Decreased metabolism

It was a very nice "fringe benefit" that there were also emotional benefits to meditation that came in the form of decreased anxiety, less depression and a more relaxed approach to life.

In 1998, I had the good fortune to enjoy a week of clinical training in stress management at the Harvard Medical School Institute of Mind-Body Medicine. Because of my recent diagnosis of high blood pressure, I was delighted when I learned a simple meditation technique that even I could do which, theoretically, could counter the physiological effects of stress. The technique, called "Respiratory One" was developed by Herbert Benson, M.D. former Associate Professor of Medicine at Harvard's Mind-Body Medical Institute, for the purpose of eliciting the body's relaxation response. The relaxation response is your body's means of reversing the physiological effects of the fight-or-flight response. While the fight-or-flight response usually occurs automatically (involuntarily) and sometimes even without our awareness, we have to consciously bring about the relaxation response. Dr. Benson was one of the first people to point out the importance of shutting down the mind's busy chatter and eliciting instead the relaxation response.

The "Respiratory One" technique, which any of us can use to consciously bring about the relaxation response in our bodies, helps us defuse the body's responses to anxiety, fear, worry and other stress-producing emotions. Your heart rate and breathing slow down, your blood pressure lowers, you use oxygen more efficiently and your sleeping improves. As an added bonus, your adrenal glands produce less cortisol and your immune function improves. Your mind also clears and your creativity increases. Pretty good payoff for so little effort!

I began practicing the "Respiratory One" meditation five times a week and quite frankly, I could hardly believe the results. Within a few months, my doctor agreed to allow me to discontinue my blood pressure medication and on my next visit, he pronounced my blood pressure within normal range. Amazing!

THE HAPPINESS BENEFITS OF MEDITATION

Researchers in the field of happiness are now recognizing that there is a strong link between meditation and happiness. In *The How of Happiness,* Dr. Sonja Lyubomirsky notes that, "Those who practiced meditation...showed increases in activity in their left prefrontal cortex, relative to the right. This particular pattern of greater brain activation in the left versus the right part of the brain is observed in happy and approach oriented individuals; thus, this finding nicely corroborating other research revealing that a series of regular meditation sessions produces greater happiness and less anxiety and depression...(It also) boosts positive mood, self-esteem and feelings of control...(Meditation augments) daily positive emotions, producing, in turn, such benefits as more savoring of the present moment, enhanced quality of relationships, more social support and a reduction in illness symptoms."

Most importantly, Dr. Lyubomirsky notes that "If the evidence was only anecdotal, I'd be skeptical, but it's based on years of empirical work. The data are persuasive that there's something powerful about this technique—if you learn to apply it with sedulous effort and commitment. Successful practitioners of meditation cultivate it like physical exercise; as a daily way of being."

Since I hold the belief that only by being my best can I give my best to the world, I consider happiness and ongoing personal development as among my highest personal goals. In addition to the concentrative "Respiratory One" meditation, I am learning to enjoy a several entirely different kind of meditations.

MINDFUL MEDITATION:
THE JOY OF BEING IN THE PRESENT MOMENT

One type of meditation that I find delightful would probably be considered a form of mindfulness meditation. It means noticing the sights, sounds, and smells around you. Mindfulness means noticing the taste and texture of each bite of food when you're eating. It means being in the present moment, fully focused and non-judgmental about what is going on around you. Keeping your mind reined in to what is happening in the moment can be quite a challenge. But, as I have discovered, it is well worth the effort. In her book, *The How of Happiness,* Dr. Sonja Lyubomirsky notes that people high in mindfulness (being attentive to the here and now) are likely to be models of positive mental health. They are typically more happy, optimistic, self-confident and satisfied with their lives. They also tend to be less likely to be depressed, angry and anxious and more likely to have positive social relationships. For some time, I have been sold on the concept of mindfulness, but I still wrestle with the key question, "How does one learn to stay focused on the here and now?" I once heard someone say, "My mind tends to act more like an untrained puppy—it just keeps wandering off to something more compelling." That's me!

Just like training that wayward puppy, I work on actually training my mind to do a "Sit. Stay" in the present moment to keep it from wandering off. I walk my dog, Abby, for one hour every morning. (She doesn't always sit and stay either!) During these walks, I practice keeping my mind in the present by staying focused on the beauty of the trees, the flowers we pass, or the formation of the clouds in the sky. My goal is to allow no negative thoughts about what may happen tomorrow or things that happened yesterday to enter my mind. Needless to say, I am not even close to mastering this art of mindfulness. But, it motivates me to know that by making this effort, I spend one hour less worrying about what the future holds and my body gets a break from the unhealthy stress hormones generated by fearful thoughts.

My mindset used to be centered around the accomplishment of the task—checking exercise off my list of things to be done that day. Mindfulness, however, requires a different mindset—one of realizing that the joy is not in the finishing of an activity. The joy of life and of all activities is in the process, in the doing. This particular life lesson (mindfulness) has been one of the most difficult for me to really internalize, but it has proven to be one of the most valuable in terms of happiness and peace of mind.

WHY IS MINDFULNESS IMPORTANT

In my experience, mindfulness impacts our lives in several positive ways: It clears your mind and gives you greater perspective, it helps people you are with feel valued, respected, appreciated and understood, and when communicating with others, being mindful and present will help you be clearer and more effective.

What gets in the way of mindfulness and being in the present moment? When you are engaged in a conversation or a task, distracting thoughts often get in the way. Distracting thoughts include things like thoughts about the past, thoughts about the future, judgments (comparisons, evaluations), mental manipulation (analyzing, ruminating), worry (pre-occupying yourself with disturbing thoughts and accomplishing nothing). A distracted mind is an obstacle to good communication and greatly diminishes your effectiveness with other people. Being mindful means that you are fully present. You have nothing else on your mind except the project or person you are with right now. When distracting thoughts intrude, you learn to drop them without allowing them to interfere. You can train yourself to be mindful, first by being aware of where your thoughts are and then by making a choice about where you want your thoughts to be. Mindfulness meditation is a great starting place if you have a desire to become more mindful, more focused and more present in your everyday life.

COMPASSION MEDITATION: A GIFT TO THE WORLD

One type of meditation that is gaining the interest of researchers at Emory University's Mind-Body Program and the University of Wisconsin-Madison is compassion meditation. Compassion meditation is based on a thousand-year old Tibetan Buddhist mind-training practice. Compassion meditation and loving-kindness meditations are similar, with both involving well-wishes for others. Many contemplative traditions speak of loving-kindness as "the wish for happiness of others" and of compassion as "the wish to relieve other's suffering.

Compassion meditation differs from other meditation forms in its focus. Basic meditation practices place emphasis on the breath and labels thoughts as "thinking," and consider them a distraction. Compassion meditation purposely places the focus on a cause, another person, animal or all sentient beings.

The University of Wisconsin News reported that recent research found that meditation centered on harnessing compassion and kindness actually affects the brain region that regulates the individual's empathy toward others. Brain circuits used to detect emotions and feelings were dramatically changed in subjects who had extensive experience practicing compassion meditation. It appears that when we place our focus on the suffering of others, our own issues are put in perspective and we become more compassionate toward ourselves as well as others. In fact, research is suggesting that these meditative practices generate responses in the brain that increase both compassion and happiness! Practicing compassion meditation, which involves regulating thoughts and emotions, does appear to hold promise for preventing many conditions associated with stress and with inflammation, including major depression, heart disease and diabetes. But it also seems to me that practicing compassion in thought and emotions might do more than contributing to the healing and well-being of one's mind and body. Since such a practice can also be beneficial in promoting more harmonious relationships of all kinds, it just might contribute mightily to the healing and well-being of the world. Contemplative meditation: The quest for connection with inner wisdom And, finally, the most unique experience for me is this: I hold the belief that it is only by stretching myself to be my best that I can give my best to the world. To that end, I insist that happiness and ongoing personal development are key components of my daily life. To that end, I am learning to enjoy an entirely different kind of meditation. The meditation that I have most recently added to my practice would probably be considered contemplative. I start each day with a twenty to thirty minute meditation. It is not yet light outside, so I light a candle and have in the background the unbelievably beautiful meditation music of violinist Daniel Kobialka. This time is a time that is sacred to me. It is the time that I put all of my ego thoughts out of my mind and focus on connecting to my Inner Being (God, my soul). I think of it as going out of my head and into my heart. I am centered, open, non-judgmental, detached from outcomes and I wait, expectantly. During this time, it is not unusual for inspired thoughts and ideas representing answers I have been seeking to appear in my mind, such as a good name for an article I am writing or the right words to convey a thought. Because of this particular blessing I keep a pad of paper handy to jot down these inspirations and then clear my mind once again and return to my meditation.

The good news about all forms of meditation is that they are free, always available, and quite effective in terms of short-term stress reduction, long term health benefits and happiness. The down side is that learning the art of meditation and practicing on a regular basis requires discipline, commitment and lots of practice. You might consider taking a class on meditation (these are becoming more and more common), visiting a "how-to" meditation website (I found several just by doing a search on "How to practice mindfulness meditation" and "How to practice compassion meditation" and so on). You can also buy a how-to CD or book, but it is difficult to read a book with your eyes closed! You give yourself a great gift, physically and emotionally, by incorporating meditation into your life on a daily basis. While you can't always get rid of the problems and stress in your life, you can allow yourself to relax and renew by quieting your mind. In doing this, you relieve tension and anxiety, uplift yourself spiritually, boost your happiness level and allow your body to start the healing process.

ACTION STEPS:

1. If you would like to try a basic meditation practice, here is the exercise developed by Dr. Herbert Benson for the purpose of eliciting the body's relaxation response. It is also the one that lowered my blood pressure. Most people who manage stress well try to practice this or similar relaxation techniques at least fifteen minutes a day.

   • Find a quiet place where you are not likely to be disturbed.

   • Sit quietly in a comfortable position with your eyes closed.

   • Relax and empty your mind of thought.

   • Inhale deeply through your nose and be aware of your breath.

   • Exhale as you say the word "one" silently.

   • Repeat this process for 15 to 20 minutes.

Note: Dr. Benson suggests that you use the word "one" for every breath, rather than trying to count your breaths, losing track and becoming stressed.

2. If you want to heighten your mindfulness and your ability to focus on the present moment, try this mindfulness meditation exercise: Take a fifteen to twenty minute walk with all your senses "tuned in." Become aware of the rhythm of your body and breathing. How many steps do you take as you are breathing in? How many steps as you breathe out? Begin to notice the world around you. Notice the trees, the grass, the flowers, the clouds. See whatever there is. Smell the smells. Hear the sounds. Try to be aware without judgment or reflection. No good or bad sounds. Just sounds. Non-judgmental awareness opens the eyes of the heart. If you find your mind

wandering, gently refocus your attention on your breath and your body. As you breathe in, you may wish to recite something like, "I breathe in calm and peacefulness." As you breathe out, you may wish to say, "I breathe out stress and tension."

3. If your goal is to increase compassion and loving-kindness in your life, an easy way to start is this:

- Sit in the meditation position, back straight, hands resting on your thighs; arms, shoulders, jaw and neck relaxed. Gaze downward with your eyelids half shut.

- Gently focus on breathing in and out, paying attention to the sensations you feel from your chest or "heart center."

- Generate a loving, accepting, kind feeling toward yourself, letting go of any mental blockages, self-judgment or self-hatred. As you breathe in and out, say the following phrase, "May I be free of mental suffering or distress." Go through the same process for any individual, animal or situation you wish to feel compassion for, substituting their name for "I."

- You can then take this practice a step further by extending compassion to your enemies and to all sentient beings.

You might enjoy this brief version of a loving-kindness/compassion meditation practice described by Dr. Joan Borysenko in her book, *It's Not the End of The World*. She provides a beautiful script in which you extend good wishes, first to yourself, then to others and then to the world. Begin with these words:

May I be filled with loving-kindness.

May I be well.

May I be peaceful and at ease.

May I be happy.

You then extend these same good wishes to individuals for whom you care deeply and who care for you by repeating the mantra substituting the word "you" for I. (i.e. May you be filled with loving-kindness; may you be well; may you be peaceful and at ease; may you be happy).

Next you extend blessings to other, more difficult people in your life, using the same mantra as above (May you be filled with loving kindness, etc).

And finally, you bring to mind all the people of the world, regardless of race, ethnicity or religious background, wishing kindness to them as you repeat the mantra, substituting the word "we" for "you," starting with, "May we be filled with loving-kindness.")

4. If your goal is contemplative meditation, you might wish to purchase a book or a CD or work with a teacher. In contemplative meditation, you want to remove all thoughts from your mind to allow a clear channel for inspiration from your inner wisdom. The ability to remain thought-free for 15 or 20 minutes does not come easily for most people. You are far more likely to experience success if you seek some form of help or role modeling.

Our pets provide us their own friendship as well.
Research has documented that pets help with human emotional
well-being by providing unconditional love,
functioning as a friend and companion while enjoying
a relationship of trust and reciprocal good will.

CHAPTER 17

Share Your Life With a Pet That Loves You

"Until one has loved an animal,
a part of their soul remains unawakened."

Anatole France

Throughout the four years of Charles' illness, I had a built in stress reliever and happiness booster. Without fail, she was (and still is) there for me whether I was happy or somewhere in between. Her name is Abby and she is an eight year old golden retriever.

Even as I am writing now, Abby is sitting by my side. Whenever I need a little mood lift, I just run my fingers through Abby's fur, and I can feel the oxytocin level rising in my body. Oxytocin is a hormone that is released into the bloodstream when you are petting or playing with your pet and is closely related to feelings of caring, love and nurturance. Researchers in Japan say that dog owners who are playing with their pets get a surge of the "love drug" which acts to dampen stress and combat depression. In her book, *For the Love of a Dog,* author and animal behaviorist, Patricia McConnell, Ph.D. notes that "oxytocin is a one-size fits all hormone, mediating love and attachment in all social relationships that involve feelings of care and connection.' It seems to me that oxytocin would be a pretty effective drug of choice, if you happen to be looking for happiness.

There is an ever growing body of research that documents the therapeutic, physiological and psychological benefits of sharing your life with a pet. At the time I got Abby as a puppy, I made a commitment to be responsible for her and that very responsibility forced me to get out and live life. When my husband died, the fact that I had Abby and was responsible for her well-being generated a lot of activity and interactions with other people that I would probably not have had otherwise. Without a pet, I might have been likely to isolate and withdraw. As it is, Abby and I are with our dog friends (two legged and four legged) every morning of the week. Even better, I never get home from a morning walk without having a half dozen conversations with other dog walkers that I wouldn't have had without a dog. Since happiness research links relationships as key components to a happy life, this is a real plus. Our pets provide us their own friendship as well. Research has documented that pets help with human emotional well-being by providing unconditional love, functioning as a friend and companion while enjoying a relationship of trust and reciprocal good will. As it turns out, the fact that our pets can't talk is a fringe benefit. The lack of language as a communication tool opens the door for a deeper form of communication that speaks to a part of us that needs to be nourished and listened to. As someone once pointed out, there is no psychiatrist in the world like a puppy licking your face. Getting Abby out for walks several times a day also ensures an increase in the amount of exercise I get, far above the level I would have exercised without her. Researchers in Great Britain recently conducted a survey that concluded that, "people with dogs exercise up to six hours more a week than those who worked out at a gym or on their own." My walks with Abby also tend to provide a beautiful connection with nature. When I am being mindful, I am focusing on the beauty of the flowers, the trees, the grass and the clouds. Worrisome thoughts are left far behind me as I thoroughly enjoy all of my many blessings right here, right now. Needless to say, this time spent with Abby is a tremendous buffer against stress, depression, and unhealthy ruminations over things that concern me. You hear many stories about how grateful people are for their animal companions, but the most dramatic change that I have seen resulting from the human-animal connection occurred with one of my dog owner friends, Dick. I didn't know Dick until he started showing up occasionally at the dog park with a little white schnauzer named Winston that he had rescued from an animal shelter. While we were all playing with our dogs, Dick would stand a long distance away and just watch. He never talked to anyone in the group, nor allowed Winston to interact with the other dogs. As time passed, some of us convinced Dick to let Winston play (Winston loved it!), but Dick continued to keep his distance (both physical and emotional). He did, however, start bringing Winston to the park on a daily basis. We kept approaching Dick (very gently) and he gradually became more at ease in our company. He told us the story about his adoption of Winston and immediately gave Winston full credit for saving his life. He explained that a year ago he had lost his wife to cancer and shortly after that, he lost his dog as well. He explained that until he got Winston, he had been so sick and so depressed that he had very little will to live. But everything began to change when Winston came on the scene. He was a high energy dog that needed a lot of exercise. Dick had remained fit despite his recent challenges and welcomed the opportunity for additional exercise. Winston had also "forced" him to begin interacting with people again. Dick showed improvement by leaps and bounds, both physically as well as mentally. He now is on very little medication and is the absolute picture of health.

We thought Dick was "in full bloom" when he invited all of us (dogs too) to his home for a birthday party, but he wasn't finished with his surprises. A few months ago, Dick, now age 82, announced that he was getting married! His bride-to-be has come to the park with Dick and Winston and we are all convinced that we are witnessing one of the best "happily ever after" stories ever—and all because of a little white dog named Winston. Stories like Dick's provide ample evidence that pets are the least expensive Western medicine there is. In 2008, Dogs Trust (the UK's largest dog welfare charity) launched its Canine Charter for Human Health. The Dogs Trust has gathered together concrete proof that dog ownership is good for our health. They compiled independent academic research from around the world which highlights these main nine areas in which owning or interacting with a dog can improve your health.

1. Dog owners make fewer visits to their doctors.

2. Owning a dog can help reduce stress and anxiety.

3. Owning a dog can help reduce blood pressure.

4. Owners who walk their dogs are healthier than non-dog owners.

5. Dogs can help the development of children with autism and children with learning difficulties.

6. Owning a dog can boost your immune system.

7. Dog owners are likely to recover quicker from heart attacks.

8. Dogs can help safeguard against depression.

9. Trained dogs can detect a variety of health conditions, including epileptic seizures and hypoglycemia.

In a survey of 1,000 UK individuals, 80% of dog owners, and 61% of non-dog owners agreed that a daily dose of dog can help reduce stress or blood pressure and 96% of dog owners and 88% of non-dog owners believe that owning a dog increases the amount of exercise you do. Staff from the Dog Trust state that "in addition to reducing loneliness and depression by providing companionship, dogs have also been shown to assist in the recovery from certain medical conditions such as heart attacks and in the development of children with learning and social difficulties." They are asking that all physicians be aware of the importance of animals in promoting human health and happiness and call on them to proactively inform their patients of the diverse ways in which dogs can improve our lives.

A few years ago, several of us who live at Wyndemere Country Club, a golfing community in Naples, Florida, compiled a book which we called, *Celebrating Life—and Sharing What We've Learned.* In a chapter of that book which we called, "Celebrating Life With Our 4-Legged Friends," we noted that if we open our eyes to the opportunity, we can learn some of our most important life lessons from dogs. These lessons are captured in such a beautiful way by author John Grogan, in this book, *Marley & Me,* as shown below: "A person can learn a lot from a dog, even a loopy one like (Marley). Marley taught me about living each day with unbridled exuberance and joy, about seizing the moment and following your heart.

He taught me to appreciate the simple things—a walk in the woods, a fresh snowfall, a nap in a shaft of winter sunlight. As he grew old and achy, he taught me about optimism in the face of adversity. Mostly, he taught me about friendship and selflessness and above all else, unwavering loyalty."

Grogan went on to state that a dog can teach us about the things that really matter in life such as loyalty, courage, devotion, simplicity and joy. And the things that do not matter, too. "A dog has no use for fancy cars or big homes or designer clothes. Status symbols mean nothing to him. A waterlogged stick will do just fine. A dog judges others not by their color or creed or class, but by who they are inside. A dog doesn't care if you are rich or poor, educated or illiterate, clever or dull. Give him your heart and he will give you his. It was really quite simple, yet we humans, so much wiser and more sophisticated, have always had trouble figuring out what really counts and what does not."

It is important to note that the benefits of the human animal bond aren't just restricted to dogs. There are many devoted pet owners enjoying the company and the benefits of spending time with cats, birds, bunnies, horses and other animals. What it really comes down to is this: Animals make us happy and it appears that they make us healthier while contributing to our overall well-being as well. At a time when many people are living by themselves and experiencing social isolation, having a pet can go along way toward enhancing well-being. While pets may cost a large amount of money due to food requirements, medical needs and toys and other pet products, the general consensus among researchers and pet owners alike is that the improvement of health and happiness seems worth the expense.

ACTION STEPS:

1. Reread this chapter.
2. Consider sharing your life with a pet that loves you.

CONCLUSION

"Happiness cannot be traveled to, owned, earned, worn or consumed.
Happiness is the spiritual experience of living every minute
with love, grace and gratitude."

Dennis Waitley

"Happiness cannot come from without. It must come from within.
It is not what we see and touch, or that which others do for us which
makes us happy; it is that which we think and feel and do,
first for the other and then for ourselves."

Helen Keller

"Thousands of candles can be lighted from a single candle and the life of the
candle will not be shortened. Happiness never decreases by being shared."

Buddha

I recently listened to a tele-seminar featuring philosopher Peter Russell. He was asked what he thought about the song entitled, *Don't Worry; Be Happy.* In the past, I was a bit turned off by that title, thinking that perhaps it sent a message that promoted irresponsibility. However, as I listened to Peter's interpretation of "don't worry; be happy," I realized that these words are actually a validation of what I have tried to convey in this book. Happiness is a choice to rise above the turmoil of the world and find instead a place of joy, peace and creativity. When we live from a state of worry and fear, we damage our health and diminish our personal power. On the other hand, being happy unconditionally is one of the first steps toward living from our highest selves. "Don't worry; be happy" is not encouraging us to ignore the world's problems; instead, it is a mandate for uplifting the world.

We are just beginning to understand the power that we have within us. We now have the knowledge and the tools to live from a place of self-awareness, self-esteem, self-love and love for others—in short, from a place of unconditional happiness and love.

We only have to use them—to put them to work in our daily lives. Is wanting to be happy selfish? Not at all. On the contrary, your happiness is your gift to the world. Go inside yourself. Find your own happiness. Cultivate it. Savor it. Spread it in the world. It's very contagious. In the words of Zen Buddhist teacher, poet and peace activist Thich Nhat Hanh, "if, in our daily life, we can smile…not only we, but everyone will profit from it."

Your thoughts shape and create your life. Your life impacts the world. If you use your thinking in a way that creates unhappiness, if you are blaming, judgmental and critical, you create more attitudes of judgment in the world. If, on the other hand, you consciously use your thinking in a way that allows you to live above the line and from a place of love and inner peace, you bring that love and peace to the world. In the words of Marianne Williamson, "The transformation of our own hearts is a necessary prelude to touching anyone else's." The choice is yours. Why wait? Be happy now!

Suggested Reading

Assaraf, J. and Smith, M. *The Answer.* New York, NY: Atria Paperback, 2008.

Benson, H. and Klipper, M. *The Relaxation Response.*
New York: Avon Books, 1976.

Borysenko, J. *Minding the Body, Mending the Mind.* Reading, MA.:
Addison-Wesley, 1987.

Borysenko, J.Z. and Dveirin, G.F. *Saying Yes To Change: Essential Wisdom for Your Journey.* Carlsbad, CA: Hay House, Inc, 2006.

Byrne, R. *The Secret.* Hillsboro, OR: Beyond Words Publishing, 2006.

Cameron, J. *The Artist's Way: A Spiritual Path to Higher Creativity.*
New York: Penguin Putnam, Inc., 1992.

Chopra, D. *The Seven Spiritual Laws of Success.* San Rafael, CA:
Amber-Allen Publishing and New World Library, 1994.

Carlson, R. *Don't Sweat the Small Stuff - - and It's All Small Stuff.*
New York: Hyperion, 1997.

Cohen, A. *A Deep Breath of Life.* Carlsbad, CA:, Hay House, Inc., 1996.

Covey, S. *The Seven Habits of Highly Effective People.*
New York: Fireside Books, 1989.

Daisy, D. *Rise Above It.* Victoria, Canada: Trafford Publishing, 2002.

Dossey, L. *Healing Words.* New York: Harper-Collins, 1993.

Dyer, W.W. *Excuses Begone!.* Carlsbad, CA: Hay House, Inc., 2009.

Frankl, V. *Man's Search for Meaning.* New York: Washington Square Press, 1959.

Gawain, S. *Creative Visualizations.* New York:Bantam Books, 1979.

H.H. The Dalai Lama and Cutler, H.D. *The Art of Happiness.* New York: Riverhead Books, 1998.

Hanh, T. N. *The Miracle of Mindfulness! A Manual on Meditation.* Boston: Beacon Press, 1976.

Hicks, E. and Hicks, J. *Ask and It Is Given.* Carlsbad, CA: Hayhouse, Inc., 2004.

Jones, L.B. *The Path: Creating Your Mission Statement for Work and for Life.* New York: Hyperion, 1996.

Kabat-Zinn, J. *Full Catastrophe Living: Using the Wisdom of Your Body and Mind to Face Stress, Pain and Illness.* New York: Delacorte Press, 1990.

Kobasa, S.C., Maddi, S.R. and Pucretti, M.C. *Personality and Exercise as Buffers in the Stress-Illness Relationship.* Journal of Behavioral Medicine, 5, 391-404. (Also referenced as Suzanne Oullette.)

Langer, E. *Mindfulness.* Reading, MA: Addison-Wesley, 1989.

Lyubomirsky, S. *The How of Happiness: A Scientific Approach to Getting the Life You Want.* London, Eng: Penguin Books, 2007.

Northrup, C. *Women's Bodies, Women's Wisdom.* New York: Bantam Books, 1998.

Orman, S. *The 9 Steps to Financial Freedom.* New York: Three Rivers Press, 1997.

Oulette, S. See reference under Kobasa, S. Richardson, C. *Take Time for Your Life.* New York: Broadway Books, 1999.

Ruiz, D.M. *The Mastery of Love.* San Rafael, CA: Amber-Allen Publishing, Inc., 1999.

Seligman, M.E.P. *Authentic Happiness.* New York, NY: The Free Press, 2002.

Tolle, Eckhart. *The Power of Now: A Guide To Spiritual Enlightenment.* Novato, CA: New World Library, and Vancouver, B.C. Canade, 1999.

LaVergne, TN USA
06 June 2010
185160LV00003B/3/P

9 780982 510933